FAUST

PART TWO

D0047524

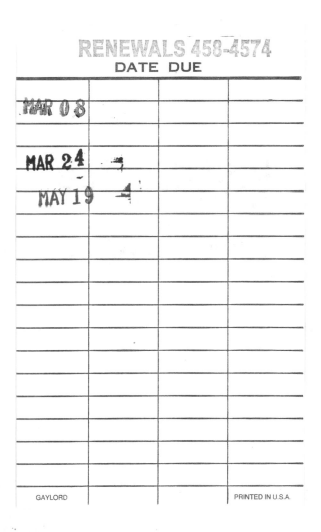

JOHANN WOLFGANG VON

Goethe

Faust

PART TWO

TRANSLATED FROM THE GERMAN

BY MARTIN GREENBERG

Yale University Press   *New Haven and London*

Printed in the United States of America.

Library of Congress Cataloging-in-Publication Data
Goethe, Johann Wolfgang von, 1749–1832.
    [Faust. 1. Theil. English]
    Faust, a tragedy. Part 1 / Johann Wolfgang von Goethe ;
    a new translation by Martin Greenberg.
      p. cm.
    ISBN 0-300-05655-9 (part 1 cloth: alk. paper)
    ISBN 0-300-05656-7 (part 1 pbk.: alk. paper)
    ISBN 0-300-06825-5 (part 2 cloth: alk. paper)
    ISBN 0-300-06826-3 (part 2 pbk.: alk. paper)
    I. Greenberg, Martin, 1918   II. Title.
PT2026.F2G77   1992
832'.6—dc20   92-13753
                                    CIP

A catalogue record for this book is available from the British Library.

The paper in this book meets the guidelines for permanence and durability
of the Committee on Production Guidelines for Book Longevity of the
Council on Library Resources.

10   9   8   7   6   5   4   3   2   1

For Gabriel, faithful reader

. . . Till old experience do attain
To something like Prophetic strain.
                                    —Milton

Earth is song and from that fount
Song pours out perpetually.
                                    —Goethe

CONTENTS

TRANSLATOR'S PREFACE

Faust: Part One ends in pity and terror with Gretchen repelling Faust's remorseful efforts to save her from execution. Behind him stands the Devil, and she has given herself up to God, the "old God" in whom Faust, a modern man, has lost belief. Gretchen's embrace of judgment and death, confirmed by a saving Voice from Above, provides a cathartic conclusion to her tragedy. A most un-Aristotelian work finds its way to a kind of Aristotelian close. The author of *Faust*, too, no longer believes in the old God; it is his voice that sounds from above, promising redemption to her soul in spite of her having drowned her newborn infant. Although Faust's love for Gretchen ends in a sordid seduction, her love for him carries him along with it, uncertainly, subordinately, into tragedy, too. But then the Devil carries him away, out of tragedy, to resume his story in *Part Two* with an unburdened conscience, his soul magically washed "clean of the horror, fright" on the very first page. This is done by the white magic of kindly nature spirits, not Mephisto's black magic. Faust's lightning rebirth is a dramatic necessity, to start the play up again—to start *him* up again as the "good man" the Lord complaisantly calls him in the Prologue in Heaven. This gives one something of a moral shock. Behind it you sense a large, a very large, Goethean tolerance. And so the Faust who awakens in the first scene of Part Two is able to declare ecstatically his intention to strive again after "highest existence always, forever" (p. 3). Nevertheless he is still bound to Mephistopheles; when he reappears later in Act I, it is as a practicer of diabolical magic.

If *Faust I* is—or rather arrives at last by "indirections" (l. 214)*

---

* Line references to *Faust: Part One* are to my own translation (Yale University Press, 1992).

at being—a tragedy, *Faust II* is what? Everything under the sun, it seems—an omnium gatherum of Western traditions, an "extravagant library," as Pietro Citati calls it, whose "books" it is possible to arrange according to the polarities and antinomies of European culture: ancient–medieval–modern; pagan–Christian–post-Christian; Northern–Mediterranean; classical–romantic; self–world; thought–action, subject-object, to name some.

Some of this is already present in *Part One*. But *Part One* narrows down dramatically to Gretchen's little world and domestic tragedy; *Part Two* expands encyclopedically to embrace the great world of Western history and culture so as to accommodate Faust's ambiguous resolution of "realizing all human possibility" (l. 1825). His ambition here is ambiguous because, like Hamlet finding the earth a sterile promontory, he has cursed life from top to bottom (ll. 1607–26); his wish to "encompass all humanity" foresees/aims at a negative end: "to shipwreck with [all mankind] when all shipwreck finally" (ll. 1793–94). Life's end is shipwreck. Yet unlike Hamlet, Faust, in the entire speech of which these lines are the conclusion, and in many other speeches, expresses a strenuous, active, ever-striving spirit that helps to win redemption for his soul when he dies (p. 239). Unlike Hamlet, too, he is not a character breathing a realized human individuality that, as puzzling, as contradictory as it may be, immediately convinces with the force of life; he is a figuration of something more abstract, more withdrawn into thought. There would seem to be a contradiction in his conception, joining as it does despair of life with tireless effort. But perhaps there isn't.

Faust's career in the great world takes in a medieval German emperor's court; an elaborate Roman-style carnival; imperial finance; a descent to a metaphysical underworld of "Mothers"; the conjuring up of Helen of Troy; the test-tube creation of a human mind; a visit to Sparta; the anniversary of Caesar's defeat of Pompey in the Battle of Pharsalia; a Classical Walpurgis Night haunted by the obscurer figures of Greek mythology (and the pre-Socratic philosophers Thales and Anaximander); an Orphic descent to the classical underworld (implied); the union of Faust with Helen begetting Euphorion, the Spirit of Poetry; Byron and modern Hellas's war of independence; a war over the rulership of the Holy Roman Empire; the expansion of European maritime trade; a great land reclamation project!

Faust II's cup runs over, its indirections seem to overwhelm all direction in a bewildering display of what is sometimes quite bizarre subject matter. So full of monsters as it is, *Part Two* itself seems a monster. Goethe scorned French Neoclassicism with its tight rules, loved Shakespeare's large indifference to such rules, but *Part Two* seems to have no rules. And not only the variety of matter bewilders, with its shifting scenes and focus; the tone bewilders, the joking tone. If ever there was a work defying all decorum, it is it. *Faust* is a very serious work. Yet so much of the business of *Part Two*—heavenly, earthly, infernal—is conducted in a manner that mocks and doesn't mock its subject matter. *Part Two*'s monsters and demons aren't frightening, its heroes, gods, and goddesses aren't tremendous. Nevertheless as Faust declares, "Awe and wonderment are man's best part" (p. 52). The mythology, demonology, and angelology, presented with amusement, have something large about them. Consider the Phorkyads, passing around their one eye and one tooth: for them we need some such category as the comic sublime. As Harold Bloom says, "None of Goethe's monsters is reduced by him; their grotesquerie retains splendor and intensity." The Chorus has an explanation for this: "Fable [by which they mean old classical myth] is more persuasive than truth [by which they mean Phorkyas's account of the boy Euphorion]" (p. 162). But that account is myth, too, new romantic myth. The end of the wonderful Classical Walpurgis Night (Act II), with the fantastic-charming manikin Homunculus, who is pure mind, smashing his bottle, his poor substitute for a body, at the feet of Galatea and spilling himself in the sea for love, with fire and water being married, with its great hurrah for Nature as Eros, inspires awe, but an awe devoid of any terror. The astonishing, brazen, burlesque-serious near-seduction of Mephisto by angelic love in *Part Two*'s penultimate Burial scene is low comedy on its diabolical side, grand opera on its angelic. The last scene of all, reaching halfway up to a Goethean heaven, deliberately sublime as it is in its use of Catholic symbols, also treats those symbols ironically, with a lurking smile.

As well as banter there is satire, of imperial pomp and greatness, of economics, politics, war, in the long first act and in Act IV; of large-scale engineering projects that are also efforts at modern revolutionary social engineering, in Act V. There is parody, reverential parody, of classical Greek drama, announced briefly in Erichtho's great speech introducing the Classical Walpurgis Night and then resumed in Act III with the reappearance of Helen. Only love detains Faust in his Mephisto-conducted tour of the world: Gretchen in *Part One*, Helen of Troy, inspiring him with the love of beauty, in *Part Two*. This second love is entirely worshipful, incorrupt, unlike what was the case with Gretchen, and begets the "petit Apollo" Euphorion. Faust loses Helen, too, but hardly tragically—operatically rather. Mephisto, a sinister figure in *Part One*, the spirit of negation, fools his way through *Part Two* and is himself made a fool of twice, by the Lamiae and then by the angels of heaven, who rob him of the dead Faust's soul. As Phorkyas he stage-manages Faust's marriage to Helen, promoting rather than corrupting it.

In the Prelude in the Theater, the Clown calls the indirections (*Irren*, strayings, ramblings) by which the poet makes for his drama's end, "pleasant" indirections (ll. 214–15). And so they are. The variety of incident and scene is as delightful as it is bewildering, giving scope to the variety and brilliance of Goethe's extraordinary poetic powers. But this has the consequence that the local interest of the shifting scenes, in which Faust is often a secondary figure or from which he is absent entirely, obscures the main dramatic interest. Take a little incident like the flood trick in Act IV by which the rival emperor's forces are overwhelmed: how amusing, how literally diverting. You don't think, till bidden to reflect on the work as a whole: one more episode in Faust's career of illusion, deceit, and crime. But then in the great fifth act, as if recalling himself to his purpose, the poet shows us the aged Faust furiously pressing forward by brute force, by black magic, his grandiose project of reclaiming waste tidal flats so as to establish paradise on earth. As his last act he again stains his hands with blood, the blood of Philemon and Baucis. Faust's life on earth ends in moral ignominy and defeat—as he predicted, in shipwreck.

In the last scene of all, however, Goethean tolerance again gives one a shock: echoing Dante's Paradise, assuming the form of divine love, it reaches down to save the unrepentant sinner's soul. Of this last scene, as Nicholas Boyle eloquently says in his commentary on *Faust: Part One*,* "We may feel that he only has earned the right to share in the vision of love in Dante's Paradise who has seen the same love in the power that laid the foundations of Dante's Hell"—the love that, commanding justice as well as mercy, judges souls according as they have done and failed to do on earth.

My aim in this translation, as in my translation of *Faust: Part One*, is to afford readers (and, I hope, hearers) something of the pleasure the work's marvelous poetry affords in the original. I have tried to cast the verse in a "language really spoken by men," according to the great Wordsworthian standard for modern poetry, avoiding as far as possible strained syntax and diction. I again principally use half-rhyme. Milton deplored the "bondage of Riming." For Goethe it was no bondage; on the contrary. But for translators of his *Faust* into English, it surely is. Half-rhyme loosens the bonds, making a natural English more possible. It also makes possible a greater fidelity to the Goethe line. I follow Goethe's meters as nearly as I can; however, in Act III, I had no hesitation in substituting pentameters for the poet's imitation of classical hexameters. English dramatic (and narrative) verse has little liking, little aptitude, for long-winded six-beat lines, which so often require padding out. With Act III's choral odes I did hesitate, wrestling with their intricate metrics till forced to admit defeat. Many of the odes have been turned into regular pentameter verse. Without the complex music they have in the German, or a substitute music, their lines in English are odes only to the eye, only as irregularly arranged lines.

I owe a large debt to those who have gone before along this long road, saving me from many a misstep, but again especially to Barker Fairley's prose translation. An eminent Goethe scholar of an earlier generation, and a writer of pure English, Professor Fairley's sardonic deflation of the turgidities of the old translations into plain speech was as amusing as it was helpful to me. Once again, too, I am pleased to

* (Cambridge University Press, 1987).

thank Professor Cyrus Hamlin for his understanding critique of the translation. I also wish to thank Laura Jones Dooley for her generous helpfulness as well as expertness in editing the manuscript and JoAnn DiCera, both of Yale University Press.

When I contemplated translating *Faust II*, what seemed its interminable length, as well as the difficulties threatened by its strangeness, gave me pause. Without the encouragement of my friend the late Irving Howe, who waved away all doubts, and the quiet confidence of my wife, Paula Fox, whose fine critical eye watched over every page of the work as it progressed, I shouldn't have undertaken it. To them I dedicate this translation.

AUST

PART TWO

ACT I

A PLEASANT LANDSCAPE

Faust stretched out in a field of flowers, tired, restless, trying to sleep.
Twilight.
Hovering about in the air, a band of graceful sprites.

ARIEL. [*Singing to the accompaniment of Aeolian harps*]
When blossoms drift down in the spring,
Showering all who live on earth,
When brown fields brighten into green,
Promising heaped harvest wealth,
Elves, tiny yet effectual,
Dart here, dart there, help where they can;
No matter who, saint, criminal,
They feel for the unfortunate man.
You airy spirits circling this prostrate figure,
Show yours is the kind, the noble elfin nature,   10
Ameliorate the cruel strife in his heart,
Pluck out self-condemnation's burning dart
And wash his soul clean of the horror, fright.
Four watches make up the slow-turning night;
Take care their hours pass benignly for him.
First lay his head on pillows of cool linen,
Then bathe him in the dews of Lethe river,
His rigid limbs will soon relax their tension
As he sleeps daywards and recovers vigor.
Your kindest office, perform it, each sprite,   20
Restore him to the blessed light!
CHORUS. [*Solo voice, duet, and full chorus, by turns*]
When the cooler evening breeze
Blows along this green-walled glade,
Then the perfumed twilight trails
Veiling mists through the brown shade,

1

Hushes man's heart like a child's,
Whispering peace, tranquillity,
On these tired, aching eyes
Softly shuts the door of day.

Darkness on the world now settles,   30
Up the sky star follows star,
Great lamps some, some flickering candles,
Glittering near, shining afar,
Here reflected in lake water,
Sparkling there in the clear sky,
And sealing all in deepest slumber
The moon in splendor thrones on high.

Now the hours of joy and pain
All are spent and passed away;
Know you will be well again,   40
Trust yourself to the new day!
Hills rise up, green vales unfold,
Bushes cast their first, cool shadows,
And the ripening fields of grain
Roll harvestwards in silver billows.

To have your every wish, desire,
Wake, regard the glorious light!
What holds you bound is a mild power,
Sleep's a shell, break out of it!
Up, no lagging, boldly does it,   50
Though the crowd doubts and delays,
All's possible to a great spirit
Who sees, and seeing's quick to seize.

[*A tremendous din announces the rising of the sun.*]

ARIEL.   Hear the Hours' loud career
Which only spirit ears can hear
As once again a new day's born!
Granite gates jar open, grating,

Apollo's car drives up, wheels rattling—
Oh what a din it makes, the dawn!
Glittering trumpets loudly blaring   60
Dazzle eyes and ears dumbfound
With sounds unheard of, past all hearing.
Creep inside a folded flower,
Under rocks and leaves, still farther,
Where all's hushed and hidden—for,
Once hearing it, you'll hear no more!

FAUST. Life pulses in me with a quickened beat,
    Drumming a welcome to the dawn's first light,
    Earth, you stood steadfast, too, through the long night
    And now breathe with new vigor at my feet,   70
    Surrounding me already with so much pleasure,
    Firing me with a purpose I'll never forswear,
    To strive after highest existence always, forever.
    Day breaks grayly, slowly the world's revealed,
    The woods ring with a thousand-throated life,
    Mist swirls and streams along steep-sided vales,
    Yet the light of heaven, falling into the gulf,
    Awakens bough and branch—they start into view
    Out of the odorous dark where they lay sleeping;
    And colors emerge from the dimness, hue on hue,   80
    On flower and leaf the pearly dew trembles, dripping.
    All around me I see a paradise appearing!

    And look up there at the giant peaks announcing
    The solemn hour at hand! They are first
    To enjoy the eternal light, which downwards creeping
    Reaches us after. Alpine meadows, a patch
    Of green, each, in the evergreen, show greener
    Still, show clearer, as step by step the light
    Descends. And there it is, the sun! But brighter
    Than eyes can bear—I avert my dazzled sight.   90

    Just so, when we have worked to realize
    Our highest hopes, what we have longed for most,

And find at last the great gate standing wide,
Out of the depths beyond, eternal, vast,
Excess of light erupts, a storm of flames,
Confounding us. We thought to light the torch
Of life, a sea of fire overwhelms
Us instead. Is it love, is it hate, the fire in which
We burn?—pain following joy, joy pain
In awful alternation, till we are forced   100
To turn back to the lowly earth again
And shelter in her veiling morning mist.

Then let the blinding sun shine at my back,
My face be turned to the sounding waterfall
Shooting down the wall of rock! The more I look,
The more delight I take seeing it roll
Down cliff and crag, into innumerable tumbling
Streamlets breaking, with bursts of bright spray flying
High in the air. How still more glorious when
The changing-unchanging bow from the watery uproar   110
Springs, the tinted arch now sharply drawn,
Now blurring and fading away in a misty shower.
The bow is a mirror of our human endeavor;
When you think about it, how clear the realization:
Our rainbow-hued life, it too's a reflection.

THE IMPERIAL PALACE

THRONE ROOM

Awaiting the Emperor, his Council of State. Trumpets. Courtiers of every kind, richly dressed, advance to front. The Emperor ascends the throne, the Astrologer on his right.

EMPEROR. My loyal subjects, welcome all,
      Assembled here from near and far!
      —I see him, my philosopher,
      But where the devil is my fool?

JUNKER. Fell straight down as if struck   120
    As he came waddling at your back.
    They lugged the tub of guts away—
    Drunk or dead? It's hard to say.
SECOND JUNKER. As if by magic, in a trice,
    There stood another in his place,
    Very elegantly dressed,
    Yet all start back, he's so grotesque.
    The watch with their crossed halberds bar
    The clown from coming through the door.
    —Well, I must say: such brazenness!   130
    Here he is, right in our midst!
MEPHISTO. [*Kneeling at the foot of the throne*]
    Who's cursed roundly, then embraced?
    Who's wished for first and then dismissed?
    Who's shielded always in his post?
    Who's scolded harshly and denounced?
    Whom mayn't you bid come again?
    Whose name is greeted with a smile?
    Who is it drawing near your throne?
    Who's sent himself into exile?
EMPEROR. Right now spare us, please, your wit,   140
    This is not the place for it.
    Riddles enough these lords here pose—
    I'd like to hear how you'd solve those!
    My old fool's gone, I fear, his final journey;
    Come here, fool, and take his place beside me.

[*Mephistopheles mounts the steps and stands at his left.*]

MUTTERINGS FROM THE CROWD.
    A new fool—New troubles, then—
    I wonder where he came from—
    However did the man get in?—
    The old fool dropped—His race was run—
    A tub he was—A stick this one.   150
EMPEROR. And so welcome, dear companions,

Gathered here from far and near!
The time's auspicious, say all omens,
Good fortune's ours, the stars declare.
But tell me why when we wish most of all
To be diverted from our nagging cares,
Back we should return to state affairs,
Lay down the grinning masks of Carnival?
Well, you admitted no objection, said
It had to be. So here we are. Proceed.   160
CHANCELLOR. The highest virtue, shining halolike
Around the Emperor's head, which only he
May make prevail by his authority,
Is—justice! What all men love, cry out for, seek
To have and sorely need—they look
To him, as loyal subjects, for it.
Yet what good is a well-intentioned heart,
Good understanding and a willing hand
When there's a fever raging through the realm
And every evil hatches out a swarm   170
Of yet more evils. Look out from where we stand,
Here on this height, across the wide land,
And what do you see? A nightmare where grotesquely
Disorder, apelike, mocks what's right and seemly,
Where lawlessness is law, new crimes old crimes outdoing,
And everywhere about us all's misrule, wrongdoing.

One man steals cattle, one the wife of his neighbor,
A third cup and candlestick from the altar,
And talks about it for years with a grin,
Never fearing the lash, safe in his skin.   180
The courthouse is crowded with plaintiffs appealing,
The judge sits high up in cushioned state,
While out in the street an angry mob, gathering,
Threatens to erupt in open revolt.
He can boast of his crimes, the insolent wretch,
Who's backed by accomplices even more wicked,

While "Guilty!" 's the verdict you hear from the bench
Where innocence has but itself to defend it.
And thus the whole world goes to smash,
All decency outraged, derided;   190
How should it thrive, then, that right sense
By which our actions must be guided?
An honest man is swayed in time
By flattering words and venal offers;
The judge who fails to punish crime
Allies himself with the evildoers.
The picture I've painted is black indeed,
I'd paint it blacker if I could. [*Pause.*]
There's no avoiding the strictest measures;
When all men injure, in turn are injured,   200
Even the throne finds it is endangered.
MINISTER OF WAR. What days of riot, murderous brawls!
All strike wildly, themselves are struck,
Deaf to all of our commands.
The burgher safe behind his walls,
The knight in his castle high on a rock
Conspire to frustrate our demands,
Withhold troops pledged His Majesty.
Our mercenaries growl impatiently,
Shout from the ranks they want their pay,   210
If we didn't owe them so much, our army
Would long ago have melted away.
It's stirring up a hornet's nest
To countermand what all are determined on;
The Reich they've sworn to defend to the last
Lies in ruins, pillaged and trampled on.
No effort's made to check these disorders,
Half the world's in a state of collapse,
And the kings around us, our neighbors,
Think, "It's got nothing to do with us."   220
TREASURER. There's just no counting on allies!
The subsidies they swore to send,

Like our piped water, never arrives.
Also, Sire, throughout the land
Who is it owns the property?
All over new men have moved in,
Barons who like their liberty,
And we stand by, looking on:
So many rights we've given away,
Not a right's left us, no, not one.   230
And as for the parties, as they're known,
It doesn't matter, their praise or blame,
They're not to be relied upon,
They love us, they hate us, it's all the same.
Guelph and Ghibelline lie low,
Resting up from their latest bout.
Who lifts a hand for his neighbor now?
Me and mine, each thinks about.
No gold's to be had, search high, search low,
All scrimp and scrape, squeeze every penny,   240
With the result our Treasury's empty.
STEWARD. The things I must contend with, too!
Daily we do our best to save,
Daily we spend more than we have,
Every day brings a new woe.
The cooks are lucky, lack no provision,
Payments in kind of boar and venison,
Rabbit, chicken, duck, goose, turkey
Come in on time or very nearly.
But as for the wine, it's been drunk up.   250
We used to have barrels stacked to the ceiling
From the best vineyards, the best years,
But now all's gone, there's not a drop
Thanks to our noble lords' endless swilling.
The Stadtrat, too, have broached their stores,
Drawing it off by bumper and bowlful
Till the banquet finishes under the table.
It's me must deal with the bills, arrears;

The Jew's unrelenting, today what I borrow
Devours the rents I look for tomorrow.   260
There's not enough time for the pigs to fatten,
The pillow's been pawned our heads rest on at night,
Bread's put on the table we've already eaten.
EMPEROR. [*After a moment's reflection, to Mephistopheles*]
    Fool, I suppose you, too, have got a complaint?
MEPHISTO. Me, Sir? No, Sir! All's so splendid here,
    Yourself, your noble court! How should there be
    A want of confidence where the Emperor
    In all things is obeyed implicitly?
    Where his power stands ready to rout all hostile force?
    Where so much goodwill, married to good sense,   270
    Loyally waits to serve him in every way?
    How should the agents of mischief succeed in combining,
    Darkness prevail, where light so effulgent is shining?
MUTTERINGS FROM THE CROWD.
        A rascal, that one—Knows all the tricks—
        Talks a good line—For as long as it works—
        You can't fool me, I see through his game—
        So what will it be?—Some grandiose scheme.
MEPHISTO. Where isn't there something lacking on this earth?
    There it's this, there it's that, here what's lacking is cash.
    You don't pick money up right off the floor;   280
    But as deep as it's buried, a wise head can find it.
    Under ancient walls, inside thick veins of ore
    The gold to be had, minted as well as unminted!
    Who is it, you ask, will dig us up this treasure?
    A clever man using the mind that's his from Nature.
CHANCELLOR. Nature! Mind! How dare you! For talking so
    We burn atheists at the stake, fellow!
    Language like that is dangerous blasphemy!
    Nature is sin, mind rank heresy;
    The two beget as their offspring   290
    The monster doubt, that misshapen thing.
    No more, you hear!—In our Empire

Two classes, orders, only are,
Which worthily uphold the throne:
The nobles one, clergy the other.
They shelter it from every storm
And their reward is bench and altar.
If the rabble in its distraction
Should ever rise up in rebellion,
You'll find behind it, make no mistake,   300
The sorcerer and heretic.
They undermine us in town and country,
And now you want, by an impudent trick,
To sneak them into this august body.
—No welcome to those wicked men!
The fool with them is close akin.
MEPHISTO. Aha, those accents! That's a man of learning.
What you can't touch, be sure it has no being,
What you can't grasp, for you it counts as nothing,
What you can't put in numbers, is a cheat,   310
What you can't weigh, well then, it has no weight,
What you don't mint yourself is counterfeit.
EMPEROR. [*To Chancellor*] Are we better off by all this arguing?
What good's all your Lenten sermonizing?
I'm sick of hearing if and when and but;
What's lacking's money, well then get me it.
MEPHISTO. I'll get you all you need, more than you need;
It's easy, though what's easy's also hard.
The stuff is there, the trick is to discover it.
So who's the one that knows the way to it?   320
Think how in those old centuries of fear
When mounted hordes descended everywhere,
How many a one, trembling with apprehension,
Buried from sight his every dearest possession.
So it was when mighty Rome held sway,
So yesterday, and so it is today.
It's all there still, in the ground where people hid it;
The ground's the Emperor's, so he should have it!

TREASURER. For a fool he doesn't speak so badly;
By ancient prerogative it's the Emperor's legally.   330
CHANCELLOR. Satan's laying golden snares to catch us;
It's not right what he says, it's not religious.
STEWARD. If he can repair the Court's budget, why quibble?
I don't mind overstepping the line a little.
MINISTER OF WAR. Wise fool! He promises each a piece of the pie.
But it's not for a soldier to mix in policy!
MEPHISTO. Perhaps you think I'm trying to take you in?
Well, here is the Astrologer—ask him!
He knows the heavens, their every star and sphere.
—Tell us, Sir: how does it look up there?   340
MUTTERINGS IN THE CROWD.
    Fool and dreamer—So near the throne—
    We're tired of hearing the same old tune—
    Scoundrels both—In cahoots—
    Sir Fool whispers—Dr. Stargazer spouts.
ASTROLOGER. [*Prompted by Mephistopheles*] The sun's pure gold, gold
    without alloy;
Quick Mercury bears messages for pay;
Frau Venus has bewitched you with her light
As sweetly she looks down, early and late;
The moon, the fickle moon, yet maidenly;
With his sword sheathed, Mars still looks threateningly;   350
But Jupiter's aspect shows best of all;
Saturn's huge but, so far off, looks small:
As metal he's not held in high repute,
Although his weight is great his value's not.
When Luna is with Sol in chaste accord,
Silver with gold, then all the world is glad!
Then all else waits by you to be possessed:
Palace and garden, pink cheek and dainty breast.
All this he can command, the learned man—
What not one of us here can do, he can!   360
EMPEROR. I hear him, hear him *twice*, distinctly;
Nevertheless he does not convince me.

MUTTERINGS IN THE CROWD.

>Astrological rubbish—Alchemy—
>Heard it so often—Hoped foolishly—
>It means nothing—Stale stuff, a joke—
>Let him show up here!—I know he's a crook.

MEPHISTO. Look at them standing there, gawping and gaping,

>Refuse to believe there's treasure waiting.
>Yet one will mumble about mandrakes,
>The black dog another—great skeptics, you see!   370
>Well, sneer away, make lots of jokes,
>Cry work of the Devil, rank sorcery—
>Till there's a prickling in your sole,
>Till losing your balance, you stumble and reel.
>It's then all feel the secret working
>Of ever ruling Nature's power,
>From the lowest depths a sense of something
>Upward steals, a tremor, shudder.
>When your every limb aches like the devil,
>When the wind blows strangely all around,   380
>Fall to at once with pick and shovel,
>The treasure's there, right where you stand!

MUTTERINGS IN THE CROWD.

>My foot feels a lead weight—
>My arm hurts—It must be gout—
>How it itches, my big toe—
>And oh my back, it aches so—
>By these signs you would swear
>A king's ransom's buried here.

EMPEROR. Then right now, fool! No sneaking off!

>Prove your words are more than froth: 390
>Lead us to the buried hoard.
>I'll lay aside scepter and sword,
>With imperial hands, if you're telling the truth,
>Dig myself. But prove a liar
>And down you go into Hellfire.

MEPHISTO. [*Aside*] Well, I should think I know the way there!

>—I can't say it often enough,

What wealth waits to be picked up.
The peasant plowing his strip of earth
Turns up with the sod a gold cup,   400
Scratching his clay walls for saltpeter,
Fearful, joyful, what does he find?
Kronen hidden under the plaster.
The vaults that beg to be unsealed!
The tunnels, crevices that wind
Down nearly to the underworld
Which he who has a nose for gold
Will dare to enter unappalled!
In cellars long closed off he'll find
Golden vessels, dishes, tankards   410
Stacked and piled and heaped up roofwards,
Ruby-crusted cups that stand
Just at the elbow. If inclined,
He can broach, from casks in rows,
Ancient vintages. However—
If you'll believe one who knows,
The staves have long since rotted away;
What keeps the wine in is its crust of tartar.
The best part of such noble liquor,
No less than gold and jewelry,   420
By preference dwells in night and gloom.
The wise man searches tirelessly;
To see by daylight, that's child's play,
But where it's dark, there mysteries have their home.
EMPEROR. Keep your mysteries, your gloom!
　　Sneak thieves go undetected in the dark,
　　At night all cats are gray, all cows are black.
　　Below us pots of gold, you claim, lie hidden—
　　All right, then plow them up, let's see them!
MEPHISTO. Take pick and shovel and dig yourself,   430
　　Work like a peasant, it's good for the health,
　　And golden calves, so many, a herd
　　Starting out of the earth, are your reward.
　　Immediately with what delight

You'll deck yourself and your mistress out.
Jewels that sparkle with every color
Lend beauty and majesty even more luster.
EMPEROR. Yes, yes! But quick! How long must we wait?
ASTROLOGER. [*As above (prompted by Mephistopheles)*]
    Sire, I beg you, restrain your eagerness!
    First we must let the Carnival season pass.   440
    Nothing can be done to any purpose
    When all are pleasure-minded, unserious.
    Penance is called for, sobriety, composure;
    Our higher strivings license our lower.
    Who craves good things, first himself be good,
    Who craves delights, tame his unruly blood,
    Who wants wine, patience till grapes ripen,
    Who hopes for miracles, his faith strengthen.
EMPEROR. Then let the time be passed in merriment,
    And when Ash Wednesday comes, more welcome it!   450
    Without delay we'll celebrate meanwhile
    Even more riotously the riotous Carnival.

                                            Trumpets. Exeunt.

MEPHISTO. Fortune goes with merit, it's his who earns it,
    A thought that never enters these fools' minds.
    If they held the Philosopher's Stone in their two hands,
    What would it mean? The Philosopher mislaid it.

A WIDE, EXTENSIVE HALL

With rooms decorated for the Carnival leading off it.

HERALD. Don't expect a carnival
    Conducted in the German style—
    Devils, clowns that whirl and prance
    And Death the Master of the dance.   460
    The watchword now is pleasure, fun!
    Our Sovereign, when he went to Rome,
    Served our pleasure and his gain:
    Over the Alps he brought back with him

Mirthfulness to his boreal kingdom.
Kneeling to kiss the Papal slipper,
He begged his right to the Imperial power,
And as he reached to seize the Crown,
He seized the Fool's Cap with it, too,
And here to us has brought it home.   470
Now all are as if born anew!
Who knows the world well, as it is,
Will pull the cap down on his ears
And look the fool and cavort crazily,
While keeping his own counsel, wisely.
Already I see people thronging,
Rushing together, back recoiling,
Knots forming here and there dissolving—
Go to it, never feeling bashful!
The world's a world of nonsense still,   480
A hundred thousand follies fill
Its cup up ever till it's brimful.
FLOWER GIRLS. [*Singing to Mandolins*]
    We wish to please, you see how smartly
    We've arrayed ourselves tonight;
    Florentine girls, young and pretty,
    Following the German court.

    In brunette locks we have tied
    Glossy blooms of every tinct;
    Silken threads and ribbons aid
    To show them off to best effect.   490

    Have we not earned, by our art,
    Your praises, Sirs? Oh, we feel sure!
    Our flowers, counterfeit,
    Blossom throughout the whole year.

    Snippets of all hues and shapes,
    Pieced together by our skill;

Jeer though you may at such scraps,
How attractive is the whole.

Pretty things to look at, we are,
Flower girls, yet modish, smart,   500
For women are disposed by Nature
To the stratagems of Art.

HERALD.

Show us, please, your baskets, girls,
With their floral treasure swelling
On your heads, in your arms!
Each shall choose what's to his liking.

With your flowers quickly make
A garden of these arbored ways!
They're worth our custom, no mistake,
These fair peddlers and their wares.   510

FLOWER GIRLS.

At this joyous flower fair
Buy, yes buy, but please, no haggling!
A few well-chosen words declare
What the buyer will be getting.

AN OLIVE BRANCH.

I don't envy any flower,
For all strife I have a horror,
It goes against my fecund nature.
I'm earth's archetypal yield,
The pledge of peace in every field.
Today it's my hope I may gladly   520
Grace a handsome head and worthy.

A GARLAND OF GOLDEN EARS OF WHEAT.

Ceres' gifts are beautiful,
Wound in garlands to adorn you;
What life requires first of all,
As ornament, how it becomes you.

A FANCIFUL WREATH.
>Mallowlike are these bright flowers,
>Moss grown, most surprisingly!
>Blooms beyond Dame Nature's powers,
>Not, though, fashion's fantasy!

A FANTASTIC BOUQUET.
>Theophrastus himself would not　　　　　　530
>Ever dare to try and name me,
>To please all people, though I may not,
>Still I hope I may please many:
>Her whose beauty I'd set off
>If she wound me in her hair,
>Her who found me fine enough
>To wear upon her heart, just there.

ROSEBUDS. [*Challenging the artificial flowers*]
>All very well, such fantasy,
>As a fashion of the day,
>Extravagantly made as never　　　　　　540
>Thing was shaped by hand of Nature,
>Grass-green stems and golden bells
>Peeping out of tumbling curls!—

>Ourselves, we're not conspicuous,
>Lucky who discover us;
>Come, however, summertime,
>Rosebuds burst into bright flame!
>Lacking them, how you would grieve!
>We promise first, then timely give
>To eye and mind and heart at once,　　　　　　550
>Under Flora's governance.

[*The Flower Girls set out their wares prettily inside the artificial arbors.*]

GARDENERS. [*Singing to lutes*]
>Flowers wound into a wreath

Binding brows, work an enchantment.
Fruits have no wish to deceive;
Taste them, that gives the enjoyment.

Sunburnt faces, smiling, offer
Cherries, peaches, fat plums—buy!
Tongue and palate, not the eye,
Judge best juiciness and flavor.

Here's ripe fruit to eat, Your Graces,   560
With smacking lips, with great gusto!
Roses are for poets' verses,
Apples must be bitten into.

Please, we ask that you allow us
Fellowship with yourselves, girls,
So that we may show our produce
Heaped high side by side with yours.

Under gay festoons and wreaths
Ornamenting the green bower
You'll find everything together,   570
Fruit and flowers, buds and leaves.

[*Singing alternately to guitars and lutes, the two choruses expose
their wares for sale in tiered rows.*]

Mother and Daughter

MOTHER.

Daughter, when you saw the light,
Prettier none than my pet,
How your face peeped pink and white
From beneath your bonnet;
Saw you all in bride's white clothed,
To the richest man betrothed,
Saw you woman wedded.

Ach, how many years have passed
By and still we wait!   580
Troops of suitors smartly dressed
Come, and then depart.
Round you swiftly whirl with one beau,
Nudge another with your elbow
As a gentle hint.

How many outings we got up, and
Parties—goodness, what work!
Playing spin-the-bottle and
Odd-man-out, with no luck.
Today's the day the fools run loose,   590
Uncross your legs, don't be a goose,
Catch yourself a young buck!

[*Pretty young girls throng in, chattering among themselves.
Fishermen with rods and birdcatchers with nets and limed twigs enter
and mingle with the girls, the men trying to catch the girls, the girls
slipping from their grasp, all of this providing opportunities for amiable
banter.*]

WOODCUTTERS. [*Entering, boisterous, hulking peasants*]
Look out there, stand clear!
Room, room, people, please!
Give way, just don't stare!
What we do is fell trees,
When they topple, take care—
Oh, the thunder, the din!
And when we lug in
The fresh-cut logs,   600
Look out for your ribs!
Do us the justice,
Fine dames, gentlemen,
To acknowledge our service:
We're crude, but without us,

What then, what then,
Though you're ever so clever?
How you would shiver,
Freeze to death without heat,
If we didn't sweat.   610

PUNCHINELLOS. [*Gawkish, almost silly*]
Oh, but you're simpletons,
Born with bent backs!
We are the smart ones,
Don't lug loads, no thanks!
Our jackets, our caps,
Our pants with bright stripes
Sit on us lightly,
And oh how delightfully
Idle we are,
Lounging along   620
As free as the air
Through the marketplace throng,
Or stop short to stare,
Screeching out to each other;
Then slip off like eels
To kick up our heels
And racket together.
Praise us or blame us,
That's perfectly fine with us.

PARASITES. [*Fawning, greedy*]
You brawny woodcutters,   630
With your fellow laborers,
The charcoal burners—
You're the ones we admire!
All our bows, our curtsies,
Eager yesses, fulsome phrases,
Now grave, now rapt faces,
As occasion requires—
What good would they do
If it were not for you?

Even Heaven's swift fire   640
Striking down with a crack,
Without logs by the stack,
Without big bags of coal,
Would nothing avail
To make the hearth flame,
By which means cooks boil,
Roast, stew, and broil!
Your true trencherman
Who licks his plate clean,
Sniffing fish, smelling meats,   650
Is inspired to feats
You'd never think possible
At his patron's long table.

DRUNKARD. [*Maudlin*]

Nothing this day can go wrong,
Wonderful I feel, so free!
Fun's the program, lively song,
Banish all care, drink with me!
Let the wine flow, what is better,
When good fellows get together?
You there, hanging back, come on!   660
Clink your glasses, every one!

She got mad, the little lady—
"Fool, in that coat, to show off!"
Called me a poor tailor's dummy
When I strutted back and forth.
Yet I drink my wine, what's better,
When good fellows get together?
Make the crystal ring, come on,
Clink your glasses, hang back none!

Me a lost soul? Never say it,   670
Look at me, I'm fine and dandy.
If the Host won't give me credit,

Hostess will, if not her, Betty.
So I drink on, nothing's better!
All you others, come, together—
Up the glasses, every one!
Good, good, that's the way it's done.

Pleasure I find where I can,
May it be so, Lord, forever!
Leave me lie here where I am,   680
I can't stand up any longer.

CHORUS.

Brothers, wine was never better!
One more toast, now, to each other!
Keep hold of your benches, hang on!
—Down he goes, he's had it, that one.

[*The Herald introduces a variety of poets: poets of nature, of court
life and chivalry, love poets both sweet and passionate. In the press of
rivalry, none lets the others speak. But one manages to utter a few words.*]

SATIRICAL POET.

What would give me the most pleasure,
Make me, as a poet, proud?
Spite these à-la-mode performers,
Write what *doesn't* please the crowd.

[*The Night and Graveyard poets beg to be excused because of the
engrossing conversation they are having with a vampire just emerged
from the tomb, the result of which might be a new style of poetry. The
Herald, perforce consenting, calls instead on Greek mythology, which
even in modern dress retains its character and charm.*]

The Graces

AGLAIA.

What we give to life is grace;   690
You for your part give with grace!

HEGEMONE.

Accept with good grace, not with poor!
How nice to get what you wished for.

EUPHROSYNE.

And in your quiet, bounded days,
With grace give thanks, with gratitude praise.
The Fates

ATROPOS.

The eldest, I; today, though, chosen
To do the spinning; it demands
Some thinking about, hard reflection,
When life's thin thread is in your hands.

So it's pliable, has softness,   700
I've looked out the best flax for it;
Drawing it to the right thickness
Needs a finger that is expert.

If pleasures are extravagant,
Exuberant and wild the sport,
Think! The yarn's strength has a limit,
Strain it too much, it will part.

CLOTHO.

Note I am in charge at present
Of the shears. The past behavior
Of our sister lacked good judgment,   710
Caused a great deal of displeasure:

Lives devoid of any good use
Spun out to the very end;
Lives full of hope, of glorious promise,
Cut short and sent underground.

But I, too, full of youthful brashness,
Have made already many an error;
To guard against my own rashness
I keep the scissors in their holder.

I'm glad to practice self-control;   720
Around I look with kindly eye.

So use the time of Carnival,
Enjoy to the full your liberty!

LACHESIS.

I alone am prudent, careful,
So I supervise the thread;
Round and round it goes, the spindle,
Never at too great a speed.

From the spindle comes the yarn,
Fingers guide it on the reel,
Making sure that it runs on   730
Smoothly, without knot or burl.

Should I ever nod, forget,
How I'd fear for you, world, then!
Hours, years add without let,
And the weaver takes the skein.

HERALD. Who our next ones are you'll never guess,
Scholars though you may be of old texts;
To look at them, who cause such wretchedness,
You'd think them quite agreeable, welcome guests.

The Furies they are, though you won't believe it—   740
Dear creatures, handsome, friendly, and so young!
But get mixed up with them and you'll regret it,
These cooing doves conceal a serpent's fang,

With poison filled. Yet since today's a time
When fools boast openly their every frailty,
They don't pretend they're angels either, own
Themselves the plague infecting town and country.

The Furies

ALECTO. A warning! Who cares? You'll still listen trustfully
To us charming kittens' flattering purrs;
Whoever's got himself a darling sweetie,   750
With our claws we'll gently scratch his ears

Till we can tell him to his face his sacred
Love has given the eye to this one and another;
That anyway she limps, is humpbacked, stupid.
He means to marry her? Not very clever!

As for the girl, her, too, we'll torture mercilessly
With how the other day he ran her down,
The cad, to this and that one, so dishonorably!
And if they make up, still, it's never the same.
MEGAERA. That's nothing! Once a couple's joined, my turn   760
    Arrives, and I know how to change their rapture,
    By whim and caprice, into galling pain;
    Natures are vincible, swayed by occasion and hour,

And no one, hugging tight the love he's wished for,
Doesn't, fool, soon languish for new bliss,
His good fortune now grown stale, familiar;
Flying the sun, he sweats to warm up ice.

An expert I am in affairs conjugal,
And know the right time for Asmodeus to appear
'To change love into jangle, squabble, quarrel—   770
In this way I wreck mankind, pair by pair.
TISIPHONE.
    My way's poison, sharp-edged daggers,
    Not sly whispers, with betrayers,
    Play around, do, break your faith,
    Know that you will come to grief.

Purest ecstasy must turn
Into gall and blackest spleen,
Bargain, beg, use every plea,
For all you've done you've got to pay.

Let none whine for forgiveness!   780
I ask judgment from the cliff,

Echo answers—listen!—Vengeance!
Who proves faithless shall not live.
HERALD. To one side, please, good ladies, gentlemen!
    Approaching now's a thing beyond your ken;
    Look there, a mountain moving, on each flank
    Carpets bravely hang, it has a head
    Furnished with curving tusks, long snaky trunk:
    A mystery!—which I know how to read.
    Mounted upon its neck, a gentle lady   790
    With a baton drives the creature smartly;
    Erect behind her, glorious, is another,
    Dazzling the eye with awe-inspiring splendor;
    On either side walk two chained noblewomen,
    One trembling with fear, the other cheerful, sanguine,
    One longing to be free, the other sure she is.
    Now let each lady speak and tell us who she is.
FEAR.
        Smoking torches, lamps, and tapers
        Dimly light the boisterous fest;
        Among these many lying faces   800
        Here am I, alas, chained fast.

        Giggling fools, out of my sight!
        Untrustworthy, grinning lot!
        All my enemies tonight
        Hound me with their secret hate.

        There's a friend turned enemy,
        I can see through his pretense!
        Another means to murder me,
        Ha, found out, away he slinks.

        Oh how I long to take flight,   810
        Run away, here, there, wherever!
        Menaced on all sides, I halt
        Between uncertainty and terror.

HOPE.

Sisters dear, I greet you all!
Though this time of Carnival
Gives you pleasure, yet we all know
Off the masks must come tomorrow.
And if revels by torchlight
Something lack of true delight,
We will saunter at our pleasure   820
In the happy days to come,
Companionably or alone,
By green bank and poppied pasture,
Resting, if we choose, or doing,
Always carefree, lacking nothing,
Forward striving, never doubting.
Every house whose door we knock on
Will extend us a warm welcome:
Somewhere, surely, there awaits us
All the best that life affords us.   830

PRUDENCE.

Hope and Fear, opposed allies,
Undermine the world with lies,
So they're kept in strictest durance.
Back, all!—you're safe thanks to Prudence!

Ruler, I, of this colossus
With his swaying, castled back;
Steadily his feet plod forwards
On the steep and narrow track.

But high up, upon his summit,
Wings outspread, the goddess, see,   840
Hawklike looking round to fly at
Every opportunity.

Glittering, splendid, bathed in glory,
All around she shoots her bright beams,

Victory's the name she's called by,
Goddess of all undertakings.

ZOILO-THERSITES. Grr, I'm just in time to tell
You you're no good, one and all.
But the one I hate especially
Is her perched up there, Victory.   850
With her wings spread to the breeze
She thinks an eagle's what she is,
Wherever she flies she is sure
Everything belongs to her.
But me—when worthy deeds are done,
I howl with rage and curse and groan.
—Raise up the low, pull down the high,
What's crooked praise, what's straight decry:
Only so I'm kept in health,
So I'd have things here on earth.   860

HERALD. For that, you whining cur, receive
The shrewdest blow my staff can give—
Now twist and turn, contort yourself!
—How quick the ugly, two-faced dwarf
Contracts into a loathsome lump!
The lump becomes an egg, and what
Do I see? Bulging, ripe,
It bursts—a pair of twins falls out,
One a bat and one a viper.
The black bat flies up to a rafter,   870
Off in the dust it crawls, the other:
They'll meet outside. I wouldn't care
To make a third with such a pair.

MUTTERING VOICES.

Come, the dancing has begun—
No! I wish I hadn't come—
Can't you feel how everywhere
Very strange things fill the air?—
Something's buzzing in my hair—
Oh my foot, there's something there—
None of us is hurt a bit—   880

But we've had an awful fright—
Ugh, those things! Now our fun's ruined—
Exactly what they had in mind.
HERALD. Since at masquerades my duty
Is the herald's, I watch duly
At the door, keeping guard
So that anything untoward
Shan't pass through to mar our pleasure;
Firm I stand and never waver.
But I've got, I fear, some bad news: 890
Entering by all the windows
Ghostly creatures in have swarmed
Here among us; I'm alarmed,
For over ghosts and sorcery
I have no authority.
The dwarf already was suspicious,
But now a worse thing from behind us
Bears down mightily upon us.
I'd like, as herald, to explain
What the devil these things mean,   900
But how explain the meaning of
Something you've no inkling of?
All of you must help me out!
—Do you see that chariot,
Four strange steeds drawing it,
Speeding swiftly through the crowd,
Yet not making it divide,
Causing no stir or confusion?
Glittering colors fill the air,
Stars float through the atmosphere—   910
It's just like a magic lantern!
Snorting loud as a storm blast,
It draws up to us at last.
Give it room! I'm scared!
BOY CHARIOTEER.   Too fast!
Coursers, slow your beating wings!
Answer the familiar reins—

When I signal stop, all stop;
When you feel the whip, speed up.
Let us honor this great palace!
Look how all here crowd around us,   920
Ring on ring, in admiration.
Herald, execute your function,
Come, before we leave, describe us
To the revelers, and name us.
As we are an allegory,
Our meaning's proclaimed plainly.
HERALD. What's your name? Well, I can't say.
How you look? All right, I'll try.
BOY CHARIOTEER. Go ahead.
HERALD.   I won't deny
You're young and also very handsome,   930
A half-grown boy, but one the women,
When you're grown, will gladly welcome;
A future Don Juan, I don't doubt,
I feel sure a born heartbreaker.
BOY CHARIOTEER. Good, that's good. You'll soon find out,
If you keep on, the riddle's happy answer.
HERALD. Eyes flashing with dark fire, locks like the night
Made vivider by a jeweled headband's luster!
And such a pretty robe that from the shoulder
Falls straight down to your sandaled foot,   940
With sparkling tinsel, a purple hem!
Too girlish, some might say—to tease.
Yet you are one whom, all the same,
The girls would only be too eager
To tutor in love's ABCS.
BOY CHARIOTEER. And what about this sumptuous figure
Resplendently seated in my car?
HERALD. He looks a king, rich as a shah.
Happy the man who wins his favor!
He's got nothing more to strive for.   950
Where there's a need, who spies it quicker?

The pleasure that he takes in giving
Means more to him than all his having.
BOY CHARIOTEER. Don't stop there, keep on, describe him
More exactly, top to bottom.
HERALD. Dignity defies description.
However, here's the way I see him:
Blooming cheeks, a generous mouth;
A face that glows with good health,
Round and beaming as the full moon;   960
On his head a jeweled turban;
His body robed in a rich gown.
And as for how he bears himself?
Kinglike—heralds know a kingly mien.
BOY CHARIOTEER. He's Plutus, he is—god of Wealth!
Come here himself in all his pompery,
The Emperor needs him urgently.
HERALD. And you, tell me who you might be?
BOY CHARIOTEER. I'm Poetry, that prodigal
Whose nature is fulfilled when he   970
Squanders lavishly on all
His inmost self, his heart and soul.
I, too, am rich, immeasurably;
My wealth, which Plutus's quite equals,
Enlivens all his feasts and revels,
What he hasn't, I supply.
HERALD. Your boasting doesn't ill become you.
Well, let's see the fine tricks you do.
BOY CHARIOTEER. Just by snapping, see, my fingers,
All around it sparkles, glitters;   980
Presto, strings of pearls appear!

[*Continuing to snap his fingers all around.*]

Golden clasps for neck and ear,
Combs and pins and diadems,
Rings set with expensive gems!
Sparks, too, sometimes I will scatter—

I long to light a fire somewhere.
HERALD. How these good people snatch and grab!
  He's nearly trampled by the mob.
  It's like a dream, how the boy's power
  Makes materialize such treasure   990
  Which left and right the people lunge for.
  —But look, now still more magic, my!
  What someone seizes eagerly
  Proves a worthless prize to him—
  The gift flies off upon the wind;
  The pearls spill from their string, transformed
  To beetles crawling on his hand;
  Away he flings them, the poor clod,
  And now they're buzzing round his head.
  Some, snatching for things solid, good,   1000
  Catch gaudy butterflies instead.
  The rascal tempts with wealth untold:
  They get what glitters, not what's gold.
BOY CHARIOTEER. Your understanding's good, I see, of masks.
  But when it comes to what's beneath, one asks
  A keener penetration than a herald's.
  But please, I mean no ill, I don't like quarrels.

[*Turning to Plutus.*]

  To you, my master, I turn now and ask:
  Didn't you confide to me the task
  Of managing your whirlwind chariot?   1010
  Don't I drive skillfully and take you straight
  To each and every place that you point out?
  By my intrepid, daring flights, don't I
  Bring back to you the palm of victory?
  As often as I've battled for you,
  Have I ever, ever failed you?
  If laurels decorate your brow,
  Who's the one you owe it to?

PLUTUS. You want a testimonial? I'll give it
    Gladly, O you spirit of my spirit.   1020
    Your actions meet my every wish,
    Rich as I am, you're more rich.
    More than all my crowns as Wealth's great god,
    I prize the branch I give you as reward,
    A garland—hear me, all!—so well deserved.
    This is my son in whom I am well pleased.
BOY CHARIOTEER. [*To the crowd*] The finest gifts at my command
    I've strewn about with lavish hand.
    From the red-hot sparks I scattered
    Little fires have been started;   1030
    The fire jumps from head to head,
    Here it burns still, there it's dead.
    Sometimes, rarely, a bright flame
    Blazes up in a brief bloom.
    With many, alas, the spark's extinguished
    Without its even being noticed.
WOMEN GABBLING.
        That one up there on the car
        Is a charlatan for sure;
        Crouched behind him's Hans the Clown—
        But so thin and wasted grown   1040
        From thirst and hunger, I must say,
        As I've not seen him till today.
        Pinch him hard, he'd never yell;
        He lacks the flesh you need to feel.
SKIN-AND-BONES. You awful women, don't you dare come near me!
    You've lost your old appreciation for me.
    When women took care of the house
    My name was Lady Avarice;
    Those were the days, and don't you doubt it:
    Lots came in, little departed.   1050
    How I guarded chest and closet—
    A deadly sin, ha, ha, they called it!

But nowadays when you fine ladies
No longer sinfully pinch pennies,
And as the case is with all debtors,
Have fewer dollars than desires,
Your husbands groan beneath their ills,
In every drawer they find new bills.
If spinning earns you pocket money,
It's spent on lovers, finery.   1060
With all your sorry friends you dine
More richly now, drink lots more wine.
So gold and still more gold I need:
My sex is changed, I am Sir Greed!

FIRST WOMAN. The creature! Let him scrimp and scrape
With all those dragon friends of his;
A hoax, a fraud, the whole thing is!
He means to stir the men all up,
They're too indulgent—I don't think!

ALL THE WOMEN.
            That skeleton! He wants a slap.   1070
            He dares to threaten us, the stick,
            With paper dragons, just imagine!
            Come on, we'll teach him a good lesson!

HERALD. My staff's raised! I'll have no fighting!
    —However, I'm not needed, see
    How all are stopped in their tracks by
    The angry monsters' hugely spreading
    Double pairs of wings and spitting
    Fire from their scaly jaws—
    Back the crowd in panic falls.   1080

[*Plutus descends from the chariot.*]

He steps down just like a king
And signals—at his motioning
The dragons lift a treasure chest
Out of the gilded chariot,
With Greediness perched on it, and

Set the box down on the ground
Before his feet. How did they do it?
It's a wonder!—I can't believe it.

PLUTUS. [*To the Charioteer*]
Now you're relieved of this too heavy burden,
You are free—off quick to your own sphere,   1090
Which isn't here! Here we're surrounded by
Such turmoil, tawdry ugliness, confusion.
But you belong where all's unclouded, where
Your trust is in yourself, your own clear eye.
To where all's good, all's beautiful you're called,
To solitude!—There, there create your world!

BOY CHARIOTEER. I value myself as your worthy envoy,
And love you as the one most kindred to me.
Where you are, Plenty pours her horn, where I,
Each feels that by it he gains gloriously.   1100
Men often hesitate, for life's contrary:
Go your way, should they, or should they go my way?
If yours, they lead a happy life of leisure;
If mine, you never see an end to all your labor.
I have no secrets, nothing is concealed,
If I so much as breathe, I stand revealed.
Goodbye. You send me off to my good fortune gladly;
But whisper once, and back in a flash you'll see me.
                                        Departs the way he came.

PLUTUS. The time has come to hand out all the treasure!
A touch to the locks with the herald's rod   1110
And they spring open! Look: red as blood,
The molten gold boils up in a bubbling river
From bronze cauldrons—it threatens to drown
Crowns and chains and rings, melting all down.

VOICES CRYING FROM THE CROWD.
Look there, and there! What riches gushing,
Filling the chest to overflowing!—
Golden bowls and goblets melting,
Out of the flux gold pieces jumping!—

New-minted ducats, so they seem,
Pour out in a glittering stream.   1120
How my heart leaps with excitement!—
The money, the money loose on the pavement,
Free for the taking! Now's your chance,
Stoop and you are rich at once.—
Lightning quick, we'll grab, we others,
The chest itself with all its treasures.

HERALD. What idiots you are! You think
The stuff is real? It's just a joke
You'll soon enough find out about.
Who gives gold away like that?   1130
Even counters made of lead
You'd take for gold in your blind greed.
Make a pretty show and you'll
Swallow it right down as real.
What's truth to you, you only crave
Gross illusion, make-believe.
—Plutus, hero of this night,
Make these people flee in fright!

PLUTUS. The staff you've got there, that will do it,
Lend it to me for a moment,   1140
I'll dip it in the boiling fire.
—Now watch out, maskers, back, retire!
What flashings, cracklings, flying sparks!
The staff's caught fire, how it smokes!
Whoever dares to crowd too close
Is pitilessly singed at once.
Now round I'll go and swing my torch.

CROWD. [*Shouting and jostling*]
Oh dear, we're dead men, that's for sure,
If we don't get out of here!—
Give way in back, space, give us space—   1150
He's spraying sparks right in my face!—
The staff hits, too, and how it hurts!—
It's the end of all of us—

Back, masqueraders, idiots!—
If only I had wings I'd soar
Up, up, out of this uproar.
PLUTUS. They've stumbled back in full retreat,
None of them, I think, 's been hurt,
Only had a little scare.
We've no longer cause to fear.   1160
But so as to be absolutely certain,
Around us I have drawn a magic curtain.
HERALD. A fine action that was, on your part!
I thank you for it, Sir, with all my heart.
PLUTUS. My excellent friend, we still need patience,
There's still the threat of acts of violence.
GREED. Well, now at last a fellow's able
To get a good look at these people.
Who's always up front, on view?—women,
Nibbling pastries, staring about them.   1170
I'm still not sunk into decrepitude,
Good-looking women, oh my, still look good!
And seeing everything today costs nothing,
I'll look around, try picking up a nice thing.
However, where there's such a crowd
It's hard to make what you say heard,
So let's see if a bit of byplay
Will put my meaning clearly, plainly.
Gestures, looks won't do the trick here,
I've got to think of something clever.   1180
I'll work the gold like wet clay, press and squeeze it;
Gold takes any shape you care to give it.
HERALD. What's he up to, that starved monkey?
Can one so skinny think he's funny?
He kneads the gold like dough to make it
Soft enough so he can shape it.
Pinch it, punch it as he will,
It remains a great lump still.
He turns to face the women, they

Shriek and shrink back in dismay,
Hands before their faces raised,
Absolutely scandalized!
The rascal's evil-minded, flippant,
It tickles him to be indecent.
I can't stand here and watch that;
Let's have my staff, I'll chase him out.

PLUTUS. He's got no notion what a storm's arriving—
It doesn't matter, all his stupid fooling.
Soon he'll be pushed aside: your staff is strong,
But stronger still an onward sweeping throng.   1200

A RIOTOUS CROWD. [*Singing*]
From hill and dale, an army, we
Press forward irresistably;
We worship our great god Pan,
Acknowledging no discipline.
We know a thing that none suspect
And crowd into the ring unchecked.

PLUTUS. I know you well, I know your great god Pan.
Oh, it's audacious, it is, what you've done.
What none suspects, is no secret from me,
And I allow you in as is my duty.   1210
Good luck to you, the best of fortune!
But unexpected, strange things happen;
You don't know what you're getting into,
Looking ahead is not what you do.

RIOTERS' SONG.
You popinjays in silks and satins,
Here we are, the rough and rude ones,
Leaping high, we race along,
A crew that's hairy-limbed and strong.

FAUNS. We're fauns, we are,
And whirl and spin,   1220
With oak leaves in
Our curly hair,
From which two pointed ears peep out;
A broad, a flat face we have got,

A snub nose, too, but never mind,
The ladies seldom prove unkind:
Even the fairest seize the chance,
When we put out our paw, to dance
With us through the checkered shade
Of the leafy woodland glade.   1230
SATYR. Hopping after, here I come,
A satyr with goat's feet I am,
Legs sinewy and thin, well suited
For bounding high upon the summit
Of rocky crags, where like a chamois
I look down on all below me.
By freedom's air exhilarated,
I scorn mankind, that dwells contented
In the lowlands' murk and mist,
Fancying their life is best—   1240
While I, on the pure heights, alone,
Breathe a world that's all my own.
GNOMES. Now our midget crew appears,
We don't care to work in pairs;
In mossy coats, with tiny lamps,
We swarm about like busy ants,
Each intent on his own business,
To and fro we zigzag, heedless
Of our fellows who likewise
Hasten on their separate ways.   1250

The Little People are our kin,
As rock surgeons we're well known;
We bleed the mountain's swollen veins
To draw the rich ore it contains;
With our miners' cheery hail
We pitch the metal down until
It's heaped high beneath the hill.
Really, we are friends to man
And wish to help him all we can;
The gold unearthed by us, however,   1260

Drives him on to steal and lecher,
The proud don't lack for iron when
They scheme how best to slaughter men.
Despise the three commandments, soon
None of them's respected, none.
It's not our fault that things are so;
We bear with it, and you must, too.

GIANTS. The wild men we, for so they call us,
Well-known in the Harz's forests;
Naked, strong, as made by nature,   1270
Each of us a huge, great creature,
With pine trees gripped in our right hands
And bulging girdles round our loins
From leaves and branches crudely made—
The pope might envy such a guard.

CHORUS OF NYMPHS. [*Encircling Pan*]
He comes!—In him
The All of earth
Is figured forth:
The Great God Pan!
You happy creatures, weave a ring   1280
Around him, swaying, fluttering!
A grave god, he is also kindly,
His wish is we should all be merry.
Under this blue, vaulted roof
He tries to keep from dropping off
Into his midday sleep; however,
The brooks run with so soft a murmur,
So soft's the whisper of the breezes
That he is overcome and dozes.
And when Pan nods in the hot noon,   1290
All the world sinks in a swoon,
No leaf stirs, the wholesome plants
Fill the air with their incense;
No nymph dares to frolic, they
Drowse arrested in their play.
But if unexpectedly

His great voice sounds fearfully,
Like thunder's growl, the storm wind's shrieking,
Then all look round them panic-stricken,
Armies turn and run hellbent,   1300
Heroes in the uproar faint.
So pay him homage, hail him, all,
Who led us to this Carnival!

DEPUTATION OF GNOMES. [*Addressing Pan*]
    When shining veins of precious ore
    Threadlike wind through rock and cleft,
    Only the divining rod
    Can trace the tortuous labyrinth.

    And there in hollowed caves we live
    And mine the riches underground
    So you, benignly, up above,   1310
    May hand out riches all around.

    But now we've found before us here
    A source of wealth so wonderful!
    It promises to give us more
    Than ever we thought possible.

    You know best how to use it,
    Take it, sir, into your keeping;
    Treasure, when the great Pan has it,
    Is a universal blessing.

PLUTUS. [*To Herald*] With steady nerves, a composed mind
        and face,   1320
    We must let happen what's about to happen—
    You've always shown yourself to be a brave man!
    A most shocking thing will soon take place,
    Which afterwards the whole world will deny;
    But note it in your minutes faithfully.

HERALD. [*Grasping the staff, which Plutus still keeps hold of*]
    Gently the dwarfs conduct great Pan
    To the fire; it boils up fiercely

From below and then sinks down,
Leaving the dark mouth yawning blankly,
Only to boil up once again.   1330
Pan, marveling, is pleased with it,
Showers of pearls fall right and left;
He bends down to peer inside—
How is it he's not afraid?
—Look, his beard has fallen in!
Whose is it, that smooth chin?
His hand goes up, concealing it.
And now a dreadful thing takes place:
The beard, afire, flies back on his face
Setting wreath and head and breast alight.   1340
All our joy has turned to pain!
The crowd runs up to douse the blaze,
But can't escape the flames themselves,
The more they beat and slap at them,
The more the flames start up again.
Engulfed in fire, a whole group
Of masqueraders is burned up.

But what's that they're saying there,
Whispering it in every ear?
O unhappy night, the sorrow   1350
You have brought on us! Tomorrow
All around the news will fly,
Multitudes will groan and cry:
"The Emperor's been burned! His courtiers, too!"
How I wish it weren't true!
I curse those who misled our monarch,
Who girdled themselves with pine branches
To roar out songs, cavort in dances,
And caused this universal havoc.

O youth, O youth, will you learn ever   1360
You must moderate your pleasure?

O Majesty, will you learn ever
Reason must consort with power?

The branch-hung halls are now alight,
Sharp tongues of fire licking at
The crossbeamed roof—the danger looms
The palace will go up in flames.
How awful, how calamitous,
Where's the one to rescue us?
A single night, no more, suffices   1370
To turn Imperial pomp to ashes.
PLUTUS. These people have had shocks enough,
What they need now's some relief.
—Staff, I order you to strike
The floor and cause the boards to quake!
You wide, embracing atmosphere,
Breathe around us cooling air!
You curling mists, clouds full of moisture,
Appear and spread your foggy cover
Over the all-devouring fire!   1380
Drizzle, showers, drenching rains, fall
On the palace, mimic woods, all.
These make-believe flames, mere pretending,
Turn them into summer lightning!
When spirits injure and abuse us,
Magic must step in to save us.

A PLEASURE GARDEN

A sunny morning.
*The Emperor, Courtiers; Faust, Mephistopheles respectably dressed
in sober clothes, both kneeling.*

FAUST. Do you forgive us, Sire, those fireworks?
EMPEROR. [*Signing them to stand*]
I'd love to see a lot more of such tricks!
Suddenly, as if I were Pluto,

The air around me burned with a red glow;   1390
Out of the dark as black as coal appeared
A rock-strewn, parching plain, and as I neared
Fierce flames by thousands from deep pits upshot
And met above to form a swaying vault;
The fiery tongues, flaming into the sky,
Made and unmade a dome incessantly.
And then through fiery columns twisting upwards
I saw long lines of people marching forwards,
In a wide circle on myself converging,
Their customary solemn homage offering.   1400
I recognized Court faces here, there, others:
I thought, "Why, I'm a prince of salamanders."
MEPHISTO. And so you are, Sir, for each element
Acknowledges your august majesty.
You've proved that fire is obedient;
Now throw yourself into the roughest sea—
At once as the tide tumbles you and swirls,
You'll find beneath your feet a floor of pearls;
Pale green waves bordered with royal purple
Heave up and down about you in a circle;   1410
A beautiful, subacqueous dwelling
Around you forms, its center. And as you move
The palace moves, its limpid walls alive
With myriad creatures swift as arrows darting
To and fro. Out of the deep rare monsters
Rush at the strange light, all in vain, none enters
The shining precincts. Dragons with gold scales
Sport in the water flailing their huge tails,
The shark, wide-jawed, gapes at you, murderous,
You laugh into his maw, impervious.   1420
As joyous as the court is that surrounds you,
Such company you've never had around you.
Nor is there any lack of lovely creatures:
Nereids, curious, come flirting their tails to stare at
The glittering palace adrift in the eternal waters,

The young ones like fishes, wanton but also quite timid,
With the older ones, wiser, behind. The news reaches Thetis:
A second Peleus captures the heart of the goddess!
And then it is yours, Sir, a seat on the top of Olympus.
EMPEROR. Keep it, that final height, only too soon   1430
    We are compelled to ascend that throne.
MEPHISTO. And as for the earth, it's already your own.
EMPEROR. What lucky fortune dropped you in our midst
    As if straight out of the Arabian Nights?
    If your imagination's fertile as Scheherazade's,
    I'll load you down with honors, rich rewards.
    Stick close to me, your magic at the ready,
    For there are times, I tell you, far too many,
    I find the daily world unbearable.
STEWARD. [*Hurrying in*] I never dreamed, Your Highness, I would
        ever   1440
    Know such delight that's mine now as the bearer
    Of news so stunning, unbelievable.
    All our debts, Sir, have been paid in full,
    The usurer's hard clutch on us is broken,
    No more must I support that hellish burden.
    What peace of mind is mine now, happiness!
    In Heaven itself there can't be greater bliss.
MINISTER OF WAR. [*Hurrying in*] A part payment's just been made the
        army,
    They're once again prepared to do their duty;
    Morale's restored, the soldiers' spirits raised,   1450
    And tarts and tapsters do a thriving trade.
EMPEROR. How my ministers come running!
    Breathing relief, their chests heaving!
    Brows unfurrowed, faces smiling!
TREASURER. [*Also making an appearance*]
    Question these two, they're the ones that did it.
FAUST. It's for the Chancellor, for him, to tell it.
CHANCELLOR. [*Coming forward slowly*]
    A glad old age is mine now, all's auspicious,

Hear what this bit of paper says—momentous!
Our outlook, once so black, is bright with promise.
[*He reads.*]
> Know all who would: This present Note is worth   1460
> A thousand Crowns. Security: the wealth
> Of untold Treasure hidden in the earth
> Of our Realm. The Bearer is assured
> Our first care will be to unearth the hoard
> Whereby this Pledge may be redeemed in gold.

EMPEROR. I smell chicanery, a great imposture!
Who dared to forge the Emperor's signature?
How is it that this crime still goes unpunished?
TREASURER. *You* signed it, Sir, last night. I am astonished
You don't remember. There you were, great Pan,   1470
The Chancellor spoke, all heard it, everyone:
"Sir, on this holiday enjoy the pleasure
Of making sure of your good people's welfare
By one stroke of the pen." You signed and then,
Quite magically, those wonder-working men
Produced a thousand copies. Wishing to share
The benefit with everyone immediately,
We stamped the entire series then and there:
Tens, thirties, fifties, hundreds, all are ready.
The joy your people feel, you can't conceive.   1480
Your city, rotting away once, half alive,
Now swarms with people carousing all the time.
Though gratefully the world pronounced your name,
Never has it rung with such acclaim,
Its letters now are our whole alphabet,
In this sign all shall prosper and be blessed.
EMPEROR. My people think it's good as gold, this stuff?
Don't protest loudly when you pay them off
In camp and court with paltry paper notes?
All right, approved—although I have my doubts.   1490
STEWARD. We tried to circulate them sparingly;
Around they went quick as you blink an eye.
The moneychangers threw their doors wide open,

For every note you lay upon the counter
You get hard cash (of course a discount's taken).
The next stop is the butcher, baker, vintner:
Half the world is busy eating, drinking,
The other half struts round in brand-new clothing;
The clothier cuts his cloth, the tailor stitches;
In taverns wine is gushing, toast follows toast   1500
"To the Emperor's health!" and cooks in kitchens roast
And boil and broil, and rattle dinner dishes.

MEPHISTO. Stroll alone on the terraces, you soon see
A lovely creature, gorgeous in finery,
Her peacock fan aflutter before her face;
A sharp, appraising eye, as bold as brass,
Sizes you up even while smirking coyly:
Perhaps this fellow's got some of that money?
And faster than smart talk, fine eloquence,
It buys you all the pleasures of romance.   1510
Forget your purses, money bags, who needs them?
Bills tuck so comfortably inside the bosom,
Folded up with perfumed billets-doux.
For the priest they are convenient, too,
Piously he slips them in his missal,
And with a lightened belt the soldier's able
To wheel about more nimbly in the battle.
Trifling matters, Sir, but not at all meant
To minimize a notable achievement.

FAUST. The great treasures that your lands contain,   1520
Buried deep inside the earth, remain
A dead mass. Your farthest estimate
Of what this wealth is worth, how it falls short!
High as winged imagination's flight is,
Nothing it is able to conceive suffices.
But minds uncommon, deep, preserved from arrogance,
Have in the infinite infinite confidence.

MEPHISTO. Paper money, unlike gold and silver,
Says what it's worth on its face, it doesn't require
Endless haggling before a person can,   1530

If he so wishes, indulge in love and wine.
You like your money hard? There's the broker's booth.
He's shut his door? Then go dig in the earth.
You decide to sell something of yours that's valuable?
The notes you're paid for it are all redeemable—
Which puts the doubting Thomases to shame.
People come to accept it, prefer it, in time,
With the result that every place in our Empire
Is well supplied with paper, gold, and treasure.

EMPEROR. We, for all the good you've done, are grateful.   1540
Your reward should be as great, if possible.
Take charge of our subterranean riches,
For who knows best their secret hiding places?
Your word decide where we should dig the earth.
Now, masters old and new of our wealth—
We call upon you to combine your forces
Whereby our upper world with our under
In happy concord may united labor.

TREASURER. Don't fear between us there'll be any friction,
I can use the help of a magician.   1550

EMPEROR. It pleases us to give all here a gift.
Tell me what use you will make of it.

A PAGE. [*Accepting bills*]
A jolly life for me, all fun and games.

ANOTHER. [*Likewise*]
I'll buy my sweetheart a gold ring and locket.

A CHAMBERLAIN. From now on I drink only the best wines.

ANOTHER. The dice have started jumping in my pocket.

A KNIGHT. [*Considering*]
I'll pay off all I owe on house and lands.

ANOTHER. It's money, so—more money in my hands.

EMPEROR. I hoped to hear bold plans for great endeavors,
But knowing you, I should have guessed your answers.   1560
It's clear: with all the wealth you now possess
You'll do just as you always do, but worse.

FOOL. [*Entering*] Handing gifts out? Don't forget your jester.

EMPEROR. Back to life? You'll spend it all on liquor.

FOOL. Magic money! I don't understand it.

EMPEROR. I believe you, seeing how you'd use it.

FOOL. You dropped some on the floor. What should I do?

EMPEROR. Pick them up, fool, they are meant for you.

Exit.

FOOL. Five thousand crowns they make—I'm flabbergasted!

MEPHISTO. O walking wineskin, are you resurrected? 1570

FOOL. It happens often, this time's the best yet.

MEPHISTO. You're panting with excitement, how you sweat!

FOOL. Look here, is all this paper really money?

MEPHISTO. You'll eat your fill with it, drink yourself silly.

FOOL. Can I buy land with it, a house and cattle?

MEPHISTO. Of course. Just bid away and you'll have all you want, all.

FOOL. A castle, too, woods to hunt in, fish in the river?

MEPHISTO. All, all!—oh, won't you make the perfect squire.

FOOL. Tonight I'll go to sleep in my own hall!

Exit.

MEPHISTO. Now where's the one to say our fool's a fool? 1580

A DARK GALLERY

Faust, Mephistopheles.

MEPHISTO. Why drag me off down these dark passageways?
    In there did you find you were bored to tears
    Among that motley crowd of courtiers?
    No chance for hoaxes and flimflammeries?

FAUST. Stop your drivel, will you, it's been years
    Since I took pleasure in those tricks of yours.
    All your running here and there incessantly
    Is just so you don't have to talk to me.
    I'm at my wits' end, don't know what to do;
    The Chamberlain insists, the Steward, too: 1590
    Produce at once, before the Emperor,
    Helen and Paris as in life they were,
    The very paragon of women, she,

Of men the very beau ideal, he.
There's no escape, the Emperor must have it.
To work! I gave my word, I've got to keep it.

MEPHISTO. To promise carelessly like that was stupid.

FAUST. It's you who showed a lack of realism
About where all those arts of yours would lead us.
First we made the man as rich as Croesus,   1600
Now we are expected to amuse him.

MEPHISTO. It's not a thing done just like that,
The way is winding, difficult.
You venture boldly onto strange terrain
And end up in an awful mess again.
Helen's ghost, you think, 's produced as easy
As we produced that ghostly paper money?
Oh no! For witches, specters, ghouls, a gnome
With a disgusting goiter, I'm your man;
But Old Nick's lady friends, though not at all bad,   1610
Could never pass for heroines of the Iliad.

FAUST. There you go again, I'm sick of it!
I never know where I am at with you.
You always find the matter's difficult,
Make new demands for everything you do.
Just mumble a few words, in the next breath
There the two would stand, as big as life.

MEPHISTO. Those old pagans are none of my business.
They've got their own Hell, not at all like ours is.
Still, there's a way.

FAUST.   Quick, let's hear it, please!   1620

MEPHISTO. How I dislike revealing mysteries!
—Goddesses there are, apart, sublime,
Their throne outside of place, outside of time.
To talk about them makes me feel uneasy.
They're called the Mothers!

FAUST. [*Startled*]   Mothers!

MEPHISTO.   You're afraid?

FAUST. The Mothers! Why, it sounds so queer, the word.

MEPHISTO. Indeed it does. For they are deities

You mortal men know nothing of, whose name
We hesitate to say. You will need
To dig down deep, so deep, to come on them.   1630
Who got us into this fix? You're to blame.
FAUST. The way, the way!
MEPHISTO.   No way! Tread, you must tread
The way not trodden, never treadable!
The way not found by asking, it's unaskable!
Ready and willing, are you, Dr. Faustus?
No locks to open, bolts to slide, from emptiness
To emptiness you'll fall, cold, shuddering.
Can you conceive such desolation, loneliness?
FAUST. I thought you'd given up such hocus-pocusing.
It's got the Witch's Kitchen's note, is what,   1640
Recalls that time of misery for me
When I lived in the world and stupidly
Studied nonsense, then that nonsense taught.
To speak the truth, as truth to me appeared,
Caused noisy protests, I was hooted down.
Such unpleasant incidents occurred
That I ran off, so as to be alone,
Into the wilds. Utterly forsaken,
I took at last the Devil for companion.
MEPHISTO. Even if you swam across the ocean,   1650
Experienced its limitless extension,
Its boundless vacancy, you'd still see wave
Following wave, and though a watery grave
Should gape and threaten you, you still would see
Something or other, a dolphin, perhaps, in the sea,
Clouds, as you sank, high in the atmosphere passing,
The sun in the day, the moon and the stars in the evening.
But in those reaches stretching emptily,
Absolutely nothing will you see,
Nor hear the sound of your own tread,   1660
Nor find whereon to lay your head.
FAUST. Don't you sound just like a mystagogue
Who bamboozles novices—you rogue!

Except you offer the exact reverse:
Nothingness—where I am to immerse
Myself so as to sharpen up my black arts,
After which you'll find me much more useful,
Just like the poor cat in the Frenchman's fable,
For snatching for you, from hot embers, chestnuts.
Still, here goes! Whatever may befall,   1670
My hope is in your Nothing to find All.
MEPHISTO. You know the Devil, I'll say that for you.
Here's something you should have before you go,
A present—it's this key.
FAUST.   That key—that's nothing.
MEPHISTO. Take it. Wait and see. Don't underrate it.
FAUST. It's growing in my hand, it's shining, flashing!
MEPHISTO. I see you're learning to appreciate it.
The key will sniff out where you want to go
And lead you to the Mothers.
FAUST. [*Shuddering*] Mothers! That word's like a blow!   1680
Why should I be so much affected by it?
MEPHISTO. Are you so narrow, hide-bound, that you fear
A new thing? Only want to hear
Things heard before? Really, there's no need,
Whatever comes, for you to feel dismayed,
Who are so used now to what's strange and queer.
FAUST. That's not for me: a soul that's frozen, shut;
Awe and wonderment are man's best part.
They cost one, in the world, those sentiments,
Yet seized by them, man feels what's great, immense.   1690
MEPHISTO. Then down, descend, or what's the same thing, rise!
Escape existing things, all that's alive,
And seek to penetrate the cloudy realms
Of empty, spectral, unsubstantial forms;
Delight in what has long ceased to exist.
They'll wind around you, those wraiths, like the mist—
Swing your key so as to keep them off.
FAUST. [*Enthusiastically*] Good, good! By clasping it I gain new
    strength,

My breast expands—on, on to the great test!
MEPHISTO. A glowing tripod, when you see it, means   1700
 You've reached the bottommost, deepest depth of things.
 By the light it casts you'll see the Mothers,
 Sitting, standing some, or walking others,
 As it may be. Formation, transformation—
 The eternal mind's eternal self-communion.
 Surrounded by the forms of all things possible,
 They see schemata only, you're invisible.
 A stout heart's needed for the peril's great,
 Approach the tripod, never hesitate,
 And touch it with the key.
 [*Faust strikes an imperious attitude with the key.*]
MEPHISTO. [*Watching him*] That's right! Oh perfect!   1710
 That way you'll have it for your faithful servant;
 By fortune calmly lifted in the air,
 Up, up, you'll rise, be brought back to us here
 Before they even notice. Once back, summon
 From out of the night the hero and heroine—
 First of all men bold enough to do it!
 It'll be done and you'll have done it.
 For by the magic's action, clouds of incense
 Will turn into a handsome god and goddess.
FAUST. But how, I'd like to know, should I begin?   1720
MEPHISTO. With all your being downwards strive. By stamping
 Your foot hard, down you'll sink, by stamping
 Your foot when below, you'll rise again.
 [*Faust stamps his foot and sinks from sight.*]
MEPHISTO. Devoutly I hope that key does the trick!
 I'm curious to see if he'll get back.

BRIGHTLY LIT HALLS

Emperor and Princes. Courtiers moving about.

CHAMBERLAIN. [*To Mephistopheles*]
 Where's the ghost show that you owe us?
 The Emperor's becoming restless.

STEWARD. A moment ago he asked about it.
Don't fail him or he'll be insulted.
MEPHISTO. But that's just why my colleague is away.   1730
The man's an expert in the operation;
He's in seclusion, working quietly,
The business needs the utmost concentration.
Calling up the Beautiful requires
The most arcane of all the arts, the philosopher's.
STEWARD. Never mind about your philosophical arts!
The Emperor's impatient, wants results.
A BLONDE. [*To Mephistopheles*]
Sir, a word. My skin, as you can see,
Is clear. But summertime, distressingly,
Brownish freckles by the hundred spoil   1740
My fair complexion. Oh, it's such a trial!
Cure me!
MEPHISTO.   How sad such a lovely thing
Is spotted like a leopard in the spring.
.Take some frogs' eggs mixed with a toad's tongue,
Distill it carefully when the moon's young,
When it's full, apply the lotion freely:
Next spring, you'll see, no spot will mar your beauty.
A BRUNETTE. What a crowd's collecting round you, fawning!
Help me, please, I've got such a lame foot;
Walking's hard for me as well as dancing,   1750
And when I bow, how clumsily I do it!
MEPHISTO. Permit me, dear, to press my foot on yours.
BRUNETTE. But that's what lovers do, out of affection.
MEPHISTO. My action means a great deal more than theirs.
Like to like, whatever the affliction!
Foot cures foot, limb limb, all scientifically.
Now watch, I'll do it—don't you do it back to me!
BRUNETTE. [*Shrieking*]
It hurts! You stamped so hard! Enough!
It felt just like a horse's hoof.
MEPHISTO. But it's cured you, see! Now you are able   1760

To dance all night, flirt, carouse, and revel
And press your lover's foot beneath the table.
A LADY. [*Pressing up*]
Let me through, I'm tortured, I am, frantic!
The rage, the boiling rage I feel inside me!
Yesterday my smile made him ecstatic,
Now her he talks with, ignores me completely.
MEPHISTO. A hard case, to be sure! But listen:
Go up to him unobtrusively,
With this lump of charcoal mark his person
Where you can, his sleeve, his cloak, his shoulder;   1770
That will make his heart throb with remorse.
Then swallow down the lump of coal at once,
And afterwards abstain from wine and water:
By nightfall he'll be sighing at your door.
LADY. Are you sure the coal won't poison me?
MEPHISTO. [*Indignant*] Do you question my authority?
For coal like this you have to travel far.
Where's it from? A burning at the stake—
We used to do more of that kind of work.
A PAGE. I'm in love. "You're too young," she said.   1780
MEPHISTO. [*Aside*] It's getting too much for me, I'm afraid.
                                        [*To the Page*]
Don't woo young ones, they will only mock you;
The well along appreciate your value.
[*Still more people crowd around him.*]
More and more! I'll drive these people off
By falling back—oh shame!—upon the truth.
But what else can I do in such a crisis?
O Mothers, Mothers, send me back my Faustus!
                                        [*Looking around.*]
The torches in the brackets have burned low,
The courtiers stand up and start to go,
Passing in orderly procession through   1790
Long corridors and distant galleries
So as to gather inside the Great Hall

That's scarcely able to contain them all.
The walls are covered with rich tapestries,
The nooks and niches filled with coats of mail.
I'll skip, I think, the usual magic spells;
A place like this—ghosts flock here of themselves.

GREAT HALL

Dim illumination. Emperor and Court already present.

HERALD. To announce the play has always been my duty;
    Tonight, however, there's some difficulty
    Because of supernatural interference,   1800
    So I must beg, good people, your indulgence:
    What's happening is so uncanny, I
    Am at a loss to explain it rationally.
    However—. Chairs and benches, as you see,
    Have been set out; the Emperor placed so that
    He's able comfortably to contemplate
    The famous battles of heroic days
    Depicted on the hanging tapestries.
    Monarch and Court are seated close around,
    The benches, filled with people, stand behind;   1810
    In the shadows shifting spectrally
    Lover sits with lover happily.
    The coughing stops, feet cease to scrape the floor,
    And since all's ready now: Spirits, appear!
                                                    [*Trumpets.*]
ASTROLOGER. Begin the play! Our Sovereign so commands!
    Walls, open up! With magic you can banish
    Every obstacle: the carpets vanish
    As if curled up by fire, the wall parts and
    Turns round, a stage appears, marvelously,
    That stretches back into the obscurity.   1820
    An eerie light that seems to have no origin
    Illuminates the scene. I mount the proscenium.   .
MEPHISTO. [*Popping up in the prompter's box*]

I'm prompter here, for your approval look;
Prompting is the Devil's rhetoric.

[*To the Astrologer*]

You understand how stars move in the sky,
You'll understand my whispers perfectly.
ASTROLOGER. Here, by magic means presented, see
An ancient temple bulking massively.
Like Atlas shouldering Heaven long ago,
Its great columns hold up, row on row,   1830
The weight of stone; two such would suffice
For bearing up the biggest edifice.
ARCHITECT. So that's what's meant by classical! I can't
Say I'm impressed. Too ponderous, too squat.
What's rude's called noble, clumsy, great.
Slim buttresses that soar into the sky,
Tall arches pointing to infinity—
These most uplift our souls, most edify.
ASTROLOGER. Greet reverentially this star-blessed time.
Let magic loose the tyranny of reason   1840
And fantasy, audacious, far-fetched, come,
For it belongs to her, this great occasion.
What all here boldly asked to see, now see it!
A thing impossible—therefore believe it.
[*Faust mounts the proscenium from the other side.*]
In priestly robes and wreath, behold: the great magician!
His exalted work now finds its consummation.
A tripod's borne up with him from below,
That's incense burning in the bowl, I know.
Next comes the invocation, all's prepared;
A fortunate conclusion is assured.   1850
FAUST. [*Grandly*] Mothers, hear me, where you throne
In limitless reaches, all alone
Yet always together! Around your head
The life-forms turn, restless but dead.
All that shone once in its pride
Stirs with the wish for life eternal;

And you, omnipotent and awful,
Part the empty shapes, to some allot
The tent of day, to some the vault of night,
Send some along life's pleasant pathways wandering,   1860
The others must be sought by fearless conjuring.
Bold wizardry is able to produce
What all men crave to see, the marvelous.
ASTROLOGER. No sooner does his bright key touch the bowl
Than a gray mist begins to fill the hall,
Streaks at first, then surging dense and cloudlike;
It spreads, piles up, thins out, divides in two.
And now behold a masterpiece of magic:
The swirling clouds make music as they go,
Sounding airy notes mysteriously!   1870
All, all around is turned to melody,
Every column, every triglyph's ringing,
Why, the whole temple, I believe, is singing!
A handsome youth out of the thinning vapor
Steps forward, treading lightly to the measure.
And now I'm done. No need to say who he is.
Where's the one don't know the handsome Paris?
A LADY. What a picture, my, of blooming youth!
SECOND LADY. As ripe and luscious as a peach, as fresh!
THIRD LADY. The finely curved, the sweet voluptuous lip!   1880
FOURTH LADY. You'd like, would you, to sip out of that cup?
FIFTH LADY. Very pretty, yes—but not refined.
SIXTH LADY. Something lacks in gracefulness, I find.
A KNIGHT. You can see the shepherd boy he was;
    Nothing princely, court-bred—wants true poise.
SECOND KNIGHT. Yes, half-naked, he looks very fine;
    But just let's see him with his armor on.
LADY. Charming how he sits down, quite demurely!
KNIGHT. You'd find it pleasant on his lap, I daresay?
ANOTHER LADY. How prettily his arm's thrown back behind him.   1890
CHAMBERLAIN. What vulgar manners! It should be forbidden.
LADY. Oh you men! With what don't you find fault!
CHAMBERLAIN. Before the Emperor to lounge like that!

LADY. The play calls for it: "Paris, seated, solus."
CHAMBERLAIN. Plays, too, should behave before His Highness.
LADY. Sleep's overtaken our pretty charmer.
CHAMBERLAIN. Who starts to snore—it's realistic drama!
YOUNG LADY. [*With delight*]
     What odor's that that's mingled with the incense,
     Gladdening my soul with its fresh fragrance?
OLDER LADY. Yes, yes, I also find the smell delicious.   1900
     It comes from him.
STILL OLDER LADY.   It is his youth in flower,
     Scattering ambrosial scent around us.
                                        [*Helen appears.*]
MEPHISTO. So there she is! Well, I am not bowled over.
     Pretty, yes, but not the type I favor.
ASTROLOGER. For once, I find, I stand before you speechless,
     Words escape me, nothing comes, I'm helpless.
     And even if I spoke with tongues of fire—!
     Beauty's praises have been sung forever,
     Who sees her falls into a trance, enraptured,
     And who possessed her was too highly honored.   1910
FAUST. Is what I see a thing seen with the eyes,
     Or Beauty's very fount and origin
     Outpouring from the depths of mind within?
     My fearful journey's gained a glorious prize.
     How nothing worth I found the world, impenetrable!
     Now I'm a priest of beauty, how desirable,
     How firmly based, how solid and enduring!
     The breath go out of me forever if
     I ever weary of you, cast you off!
     That lovely form I once found so enchanting   1920
     When I beheld it in the magic glass,
     Beside such beauty were a shadow, nothing.
     To you I owe all of my vital force,
     My passion's very heart and soul, to you
     I give myself entirely, in affection,
     Love, in worship, yes, in madness, too!
MEPHISTO. [*From the prompter's box*]

Calm down, calm down, remember your role here!
OLDER LADY. Tall. Good figure. But her head's too little.
YOUNG LADY. Just see those feet. Could they be clumsier?
DIPLOMAT. To me she seems like a grande dame, quite regal,   1930
   And beautiful—her beauty has no equal.
COURTIER. Slowly she goes toward him, very softly.
LADY. Beside his pure youth, doesn't she look ugly!
POET. He glows, illuminated by her beauty.
LADY. Like Luna and Endymion in the painting!
POET. Yes, yes! The goddess, as it seems, descending
   From above—and bends to drink his breath.
   A kiss. His cup is full—oh, lucky youth!
DUENNA. In front of everybody, I declare!
FAUST. A boy to be so favored!
MEPHISTO.   Silence there!   1940
   She'll do what pleases her, don't interfere.
COURTIER. Off she tiptoes and he starts awake.
LADY. I knew it—see how she is looking back.
COURTIER. He's thunderstruck—a marvel, extraordinary!
LADY. For her no marvel, a familiar story.
COURTIER. Now she is turning back, so modestly.
LADY. She's making plans for him, that's plain to see.
   Men, men, what fools, what simpletons you are!
   The fellow thinks he is the first, ha, ha!
KNIGHT. She's noble, queenly, don't you criticize her.   1950
LADY. The trollop! Doing what she did—so vulgar!
PAGE. Oh how I wish I stood in that man's shoes!
COURTIER. Who, tempted by her, ever would refuse?
LADY. That article has been around, I fear,
   It's looking shabby, faded, quite threadbare.
SECOND LADY. At ten already she was on the downgrade.
KNIGHT. You take the best that fortune may afford you.
   With such leavings I'd think I was well paid.
PEDANT. I see her clearly, but I have to tell you
   I can't be certain she is the right Helen—   1960
   One's judgment's clouded by a living presence.
   Above all else I hold by what's been written,

And studying it, I find that it says plainly
She always pleased Troy's ancients mightily,
Which seems to fit the facts here perfectly:
I'm not young, and yet she's pleasing to me.
ASTROLOGER. A boy no more, a glorious hero, daring,
He seizes her, her protests count for nothing.
His arms, grown stalwart, catch her ripeness up—
Will he abduct her?
FAUST.   Fool, what madness, stop!   1970
How dare you? Hear me, put her down at once!
MEPHISTO. It's you, I thought, arranged this weird séance.
ASTROLOGER. Excuse me, but from what I've seen, I'd say
The Rape of Helen is the title of this play.
FAUST. Rape! I'm nothing here? Rape, if you please!
Don't you see this key still in my hand
That steered me through tumultuous waves, great seas
Of utter solitude, to reach firm land?
Here I can plant my feet, securely stand,
Here all about me are realities   1980
Enabling my spirit boldly to contend
With spirits, and heroically create
The great, the double realm it's always sought.
So far away once, could she now be closer?
If I rescue her she's mine twice over.
Then risk it! Mothers, Mothers, let me have her!
When once you've seen her you can't live without her.
ASTROLOGER. Whatever are you doing, Faust, O Faust?
He's seized her, he has, now she's fading fast.
The key's aimed at the youth—oh no! oh no!—   1990
And touches him!—It's any second now!

[*An explosion. Faust is knocked flat. The spirits vanish in smoke.*]

MEPHISTO. [*Slinging Faust across his shoulder*]
A fine business! Never fool with fools,
For even Satan in the end will lose.

[*Darkness, tumult.*]

ACT II

A HIGH, NARROW, VAULTED GOTHIC ROOM

Faust's old study, and still unchanged.

MEPHISTO. [*Entering from behind a curtain; as he raises it and looks
back, Faust is seen lying prostrate on an old-fashioned bed*]
Lie there, poor beguiled wretch, trussed
In bonds of love not soon unloosed!
Whom Helen's beauty paralyzes,
He doesn't soon regain his senses.
      [*Looking around him.*]
I look around me and I see
All's just the way it was before.
The stained-glass window's dimmer, certainly,   2000
And there are lots more cobwebs everywhere,
The inkwell's dry, the paper sere,
But everything is as it used to be.
Why, even the pen's still on the table
Faust used to sign up with the Devil;
There's still a trace high up the stem
Of the drop of blood I got from him—
A find indeed for the collector who
Gets hold of such a unique curio!
Look: dangling from its hook his old fur cloak,   2010
Reminding me of every fancy, joke,
I planted in that poor boy's brain,
Notions, I bet, though he's grown a man,
He still nourishes himself upon.
Really, I'm inclined, wrapped in that gown,
To play the professor once again and pompously
Declare all things are as I say, infallibly,

Which your professor knows so well to do;
The Devil lost the trick of it some time ago.

[*He gives the furred gown a shake, and crickets, beetles, and moths fly out.*]

CHORUS OF INSECTS.

> Oh welcome, dear Father,　　　　　　　　　　　2020
> The lord of us flies!
> We buzz and we flutter
> With never a pause.
> You secretly planted us
> One at a time,
> Now thousands and more of us
> Whirr round and round.
> Lice in a fur collar
> Hide deep out of sight,
> But the Devil hides deeper　　　　　　　　　　2030
> By far, in man's heart.

MEPHISTO. Such a glad surprise—all these are my creation!
Only sow, you'll reap at the right season.
A last shake let me give to this old pelt;
Here and there a few more flutter out.
—Now off with you, my dears, don't ever linger!
Go hide yourself in every dusty corner,
Over there inside those rotting chests,
Here inside these mildewed manuscripts,
Among the fragments of old pots and bowls,　　　2040
Inside the staring sockets of those skulls.
Amid such ruination, rot, and rust
Queer things breed, in the brain as well as the dust.
　　　　　　　　　[*Slips into the gown.*]
Once more I don, old coat, your dignity,
Again I am the Dean of the Faculty!
How fine that title is, but where's the profit
If not a soul's around to recognize it?

[*He pulls the bell, which rings with such a loud, explosive sound that the corridors quake and the doors fly open.*]

A FAMULUS. [*Stumbling down the long, dark corridor*]
  What a noise! It's terrifying!
  Stairs are rocking, stone walls swaying,
  Through the painted panes I see   2050
  Lightning flashing luridly,
  Pavement cracks and ceiling shudders,
  Sending rubble down in showers.
  Magically that bolted door
  Is burst open, hangs ajar!
  Horrors, what is that in there?
  A giant wearing Faust's old fur!
  With a look he waves me over,
  My poor legs are turned to rubber.
  Take to my heels, should I, or stay?   2060
  I'm scared of what's awaiting me!
MEPHISTO. [*Motioning to him*] Come here, my friend. Your name is
  Nicodemus?
FAMULUS. Oh yes, Your Honor, yes, it is! —*Oremus!*
MEPHISTO. Enough of that!
FAMULUS.   I'm so glad you know me.
MEPHISTO. Yes, I do. Much older now, I see,
  Yet still the student, everlastingly.
  What else can he do, your man of learning,
  But study, study, keep on studying?
  He builds his house of cards with oh what labor,
  But does the genius ever finish? Never.   2070
  However, he's a brainy one, your master,
  The well-known, much revered Herr Dr. Wagner.
  In the learned world he is a leading light,
  Without him it would simply fall apart.
  Thanks to him each day the world knows more;
  Around him students gather by the score,

They hang on every word that his lips utter.
He's keeper of the keys, just like St. Peter,
Both to the higher world and to the lower.
His intellect's so keen, shines with such brilliance,   2080
All reputations pale in that effulgence.
Even Faust's name has been overshadowed;
All that we know, he only has discovered.
FAMULUS. Allow me, dear sir, if I may,
To disagree with what you say.
He's not the kind of man that you suggest;
Name all his traits, and modesty stands first.
Faust's vanishing so unaccountably
Is not a thing he's able easily
To reconcile himself to. Every day   2090
He prays the Lord the great man may return;
Only then will he feel right again.
This room's just as it was the day
That Dr. Faustus went away,
It still awaits its ancient master.
It needed all my courage, Sir, to enter.
—The time's so strange, what have the stars in store?
The very walls seem terror stricken,
The doorposts shook, the bolts burst open,
Or you, Sir, never would be standing here.   2100
MEPHISTO. Where has Wagner stuck himself away?
Lead me there or bring him here to me!
FAMULUS. Oh, I don't know, Sir, if I dare;
So very strict his orders were.
The great work that he has in hand
Requires him to live for months on end
In solitude. Though so refined a scholar,
He now looks like a charcoal burner
With a face that's black from ear to ear
And bloodshot eyes from blowing up the fire.   2110
A minute wasted and he's driven frantic;

The clashing of the tongs to him's pure music.
MEPHISTO. So he won't see me? I'm the very one
To speed the good work of his project on.

[*Exit Famulus. With great dignity, Mephistopheles seats himself.*]

No sooner do I settle into place
Along comes someone with a well-known face—
A B.A. now and with advanced opinions;
There'll be no limits, none, to his pretensions.
BACCALAUREUS. [*Striding down the corridor*]
    Every door's wide open here,
    Letting in, thank God, some air   2120
    Where all is dry rot, fustiness,
    Where life's not life but a slow death.
    It gives a fellow hope he may
    Do more than breathe dust, waste away.

    The walls are swaying, they're about
    To topple over and fall flat.
    If I'm not careful, promptly leave,
    I'll find myself buried alive.
    I'm brave as any, even braver,
    But I stop here, I'll go no farther.   2130

    But what's this I am looking at?
    I swear it is the very spot
    Where I arrived, so long ago,
    A naive freshman, keen to know
    All the old heads had to teach.
    How I drank in their gibberish!

    From those old, thick-bound tomes of theirs
    The lies they stuffed my young head with,
    Knowing full well they were lies,
    Stifling mine and their souls both.   2140

Look! Inside the study someone
'S sitting in the dark, half hidden.
Coming closer, my eyes popping,
I see it's him in his old wrapping,
His fur-lined robe, just as he wore it
The last time that I saw him in it.
He seemed to me a fount of wisdom
In those old days—I didn't know him.
But now I see right through the man!
I'll have myself a go at him.   2150

Unless, old Sir, you lack the strength to hold
Your bent, bald head above the cloudy tide
Of Lethe's drowsy stream, in me behold
Your former pupil, now outgrown the rod!
You're just as I remember you, exactly;
Myself, however, you'll find changed completely.
MEPHISTO. I'm glad it fetched you here, my bell.
I held you then in some esteem;
The grub and chrysalis foretell
The brilliant butterfly to come.   2160
You took in your curls and lace collar
A childish pleasure, I remember.
You never wore, did you, the pigtail?
Today I see your hair's cut short.
You look so resolute, so able;
But one must not be absolute.
BACCALAUREUS. Old man, here all's just as it was before,
But times have changed, don't you forget it, please,
So spare me professorial ironies;
We're not the innocents that we once were.   2170
No wit was needed to mock guileless boys,
But that's all past, today no one would dare.
MEPHISTO. Tell the young the plain truth honestly,
They close their ears, they have no wish to hear it.

But when on their own hides as by and by
They feel its sting and come at last to know it,
They all think it is their brains found it out.
And their old master? What an idiot!

BACCALAUREUS. Or rather rogue! Is there anywhere
A teacher who says how things truly are?   2180
They praise, they blame, as seems expedient,
Beam brightly, frown—the poor trusting student!

MEPHISTO. Well, there's a time to learn, but I can see
You're ready now to go on and teach others.
In all these months and years that have gone by,
The rich experiences you must have gathered!

BACCALAUREUS. Experience! Why, it's just dust and bones
Compared with what the mind of man contains.
Admit it: all your hard-won learning, knowledge,
What is it? Just a lot of useless baggage.   2190

MEPHISTO. [*After a pause*] Yes, I've suspected it. How stupid,
How trivial my thinking's been, how vapid.

BACCALAUREUS. Oh very good! Now you are talking sense—
The first old-timer with intelligence.

MEPHISTO. I searched for golden treasure in the ground,
Contemptible, base coal was what I found.

BACCALAUREUS. Confess it, your bald head is no more worth
Than that old hollow skull upon the shelf.

MEPHISTO. [*Cheerfully*] You've no idea how rude you are, I see.

BACCALAUREUS. To be polite, in German, is to lie.   2200

MEPHISTO. [*Who has been rolling his wheeled chair nearer and nearer
        the foot of the stage, addressing the audience*]
I can hardly breathe or see up here.
Is there any room for me down there?

BACCALAUREUS. What nerve, so as to hang on a while longer,
To claim you matter still, when all is past and over.
What's life? It's blood, and where, I'd like to know,
Does blood, unless in youth, more freshly flow?
In youth blood's vigorous, it throbs and beats,
From its own vital force new life creates,

It's active, stirring, makes things move along,
Rejects the weak, gives first place to the strong.   2210
While we've been conquering half the world, tell me
What have you done? —You've dreamt your life away
Nodding over this scheme, that scheme, and another.
It's a fact: old age is a cold fever,
An ague, full of fussiness and worry.
You're good as dead when you are over thirty.
That's when you should be done away with promptly.
MEPHISTO. About all that the Devil has no comment.
BACCALAUREUS. The Devil by *my* will exists, through me.
MEPHISTO. [*Aside*] He'll lay you by the heels though, presently.   2220
BACCALAUREUS. Youth's noblest, loftiest calling, listen, hear it:
There was no world until by me created.
I led the beaming sun out of the sea,
I launched the moon upon her changing course;
The day appeared, all garlanded, for me,
The earth grew green and lived in my embrace;
Upon my sign, in that creating night,
The stars, unveiled, shone gloriously bright.
Who but me unloosed your captive minds
From their confinement in philistine bonds?   2230
Free as the air, just as the spirit prompts me,
I joy to follow where my soul's light leads me;
I speed along in sheerest self-delight,
Brightness before and at my back the night.

Exit.

MEPHISTO. Go thy ways, rare genius, in your glory!
How chagrined you'd be to know
There's nothing wise and nothing silly
Wasn't thought of long ago.
—But I don't think he'll do us any harm,
In a few years he'll sing another tune.   2240
The juice may seethe and sputter in the vat,
Time passes and good wine is the result.

[*To the younger members of the audience, who have refrained from applauding.*]

My words, I notice, leave you cold.
Well, never mind, you're all good children.
Remember that the Devil's old,
When you're old, too, you'll understand him.

A LABORATORY

In the medieval style, filled with cumbersome, intricate equipment designed for the most fantastic purposes.

WAGNER. [*At the furnace*] The fateful bell shakes with its boom
    The sooty walls of the dim room.
    This state of tense suspense must soon
    Be ended and the outcome known.   2250
    The darkness lightens bit by bit;
    Deep inside the crystal vial
    Something glows like a live coal,
    Like the loveliest carbuncle,
    Sending through the dark its sparkle.
    I see a clear white light appearing!
    If only this time I succeed!
    —Oh God, why is that doorlatch rattling?
MEPHISTO. [*Entering*] Greetings, Sir—don't be afraid.
WAGNER. [*Nervously*] Greetings, yes—at this momentous
      juncture.   2260
    [*Softly*] But not a word, please, not a whisper.
    A mighty work is nearing its completion.
MEPHISTO. [*Lowering his voice*]
    What mighty work?
WAGNER. [*Whispering*]   A man's creation.
MEPHISTO. No! Have you two lovers snugly
    Tucked up there inside that chimney?
WAGNER. God forbid! The old way we were made
    Was quite impossible—so crude.

The tender source from which sprang all of life,
The sweet force pressing outward from within,
Which took and gave, making itself again   2270
With all that it absorbed into itself
Of like and unlike from nearby, far off,
According to old Nature's antique plan—
Well, it's deposed, no longer will we honor it;
Beasts of the field may still take pleasure in it,
But man, endowed so nobly, must henceforth
Use nobler, higher means to make himself.
                                    [*Turning to the furnace.*]
Look how it shines! Now we can hope it's possible,
By mixing together every kind of material—
For everything depends upon the mixture—   2280
To make out of the mixture human matter;
Then sealing up all in a limbec carefully,
We redistill the contents thoroughly,
To find at last all's been accomplished quietly.
                                [*Turning again to the furnace.*]
It's working! See the mass stir, brighter, clearer!
I feel more confident in my belief than ever.
What once we lauded as great Nature's mystery,
We dare to do now by proceeding rationally;
Her way of working was organic, vital,
We synthesize men inside a glass bottle.   2290
MEPHISTO. A man lives long enough, he learns a lot,
He's seen the world, he is surprised by nothing;
Already in my traveling about
I've come on more than one synthetic being.
WAGNER. [*Who has never taken his eyes off the vial*]
It rises, shines, agglomerates,
A minute more and it is done.
A great idea seems mad at first,
But in the end the day must come
When hit-and-miss ways of begetting life
Will only stimulate our mirth,   2300

When, banished chance and accidents,
A thinking man may make a brain that thinks.
                    [*Ecstatically observing the vial.*]
The glass chimes, oh how dulcet-strong its ringing!
It clouds, it clears—yes, yes, it's happening!
I see the delicate outline within
Of something gesturing, a manikin!
Well, there you have it, who can ask for more?
The secret now's no secret any more.
Hear how that sound becomes a human voice
That's able to form words and speak to us.   2310
HOMUNCULUS. [*Addressing Wagner from the vial*]
How are you, dearest parent? That was something, my!
Come, take me to your bosom tenderly.
But gently, lest the glass break in your hand!
For so things are, I'm sure you'll understand:
The universe, though big enough
Is hardly able to contain
All of Nature's sprawling wealth,
But manmade life needs to be sealed up tight.
                            [*To Mephistopheles*]
It's Cousin Rascal I see, am I right?
You've come, I must say, very opportunely.   2320
It's our good luck, I thank you most sincerely.
I'm alive so I must have activity,
I need to buckle down to work immediately,
And you are just the one knows how to help me.
WAGNER. One word more! The times I've blushed for shame
To find myself unable to explain
The problems with which young and old besiege me.
For instance: no one comprehends, not even dimly,
How body and soul should fit so well together,
Cling so close a knife can't pass between them,   2330
And yet they're always bickering with each other.
And then—
MEPHISTO.   Hold on! I'd rather put this question:

Why is it man and wife don't get on better?
My friend, give up, you'll never find the answer.
—But there's work here for him to do, our midget.
HOMUNCULUS. Work? There's work? Direct me to it.
MEPHISTO. [*Pointing to the side door*]
Look there. Now show us what your talents are.
WAGNER. [*Still staring into the vial*]
Such a darling boy you are, a dear!
[*The side door opens, showing Faust recumbent on the bed.*]
HOMUNCULUS. [*Astonished*] Hm, significant!

[*The vial escapes Wagner's hands and hovers over Faust, shedding its light on him.*]

So beautiful a scene!
I see a pool, trees round it as a screen,   2340
With girls undressing, all so very lovely,
And lovelier still in their naked beauty.
But one stands out more radiant than the rest,
Sprung from the gods or an heroic race.
She dips a foot in the transparent glitter,
Cooling the glowing life in her white limbs
In the yielding crystal of the quiet water.
—But what's that thunder of fast-beating wings?
That plunging, splashing, splintering of the mirror?
The women flee in fear, but she, the queen,   2350
Is unalarmed and looks serenely on,
And with a woman's pride, a woman's pleasure,
Observes the swan prince nestling at her knees,
Submissive yet insistent, familiar and at ease.
But suddenly a mist arising, no more's seen
Of this most charming, most enchanting scene.
MEPHISTO. The stories, really, you've got up your sleeve!
So little, yet the things you do imagine!
I see nothing.
HOMUNCULUS.   Which I well believe.
A Northerner grown up in the wild confusion   2360

Of chivalry and priestcraft, those dark times,
You lack an eye for Mediterranean scenes,
Can only feel at home in cold and darkness.

[*Looking around.*]

Dingy buildings, damp, decayed, and joyless,
Pointed arches, Gothic gimcracks—dreadful!
If that one there wakes up we'll have our hands full,
He'll die right on the spot, it's all so awful.
Swans and naked beauties in a stream,
That's what his soul reached for in his dream,
But here how could he ever stand it?   2370
I'm at home no matter where I am,
Yet I myself can hardly bear it.
You've got to move him.

MEPHISTO.   Gladly, just say where.

HOMUNCULUS. Send a soldier off to war,
   Take a young girl to the dance,
   And everything's as it should be.
   Just now it has occurred to me
   That by a very happy chance
   It's Classical Walpurgis Night—
   Just right for him, for him his element.   2380

MEPHISTO. I never heard of any such event.

HOMUNCULUS. Of course not. All you know about
   Are your romantic phantoms, but
   Genuine ghosts, the true goods, you'll
   Find are antique first of all.

MEPHISTO. All right, so which way lies our route?
   Classical colleagues—what a thought!

HOMUNCULUS. The northwest, Satan, is your stamping ground,
   The southeast's the direction we are bound.
   Through a great plain, through thicket and through
      grove,   2390
   Peneios flows along still, sultry reaches;
   The plain extends back to the mountain gorges,
   And old and new Pharsalus lie above.

MEPHISTO. Spare me that, that's ancient history!

A contest between tyranny and slavery.
It bores me stiff: no sooner one war's done
They start another one right up again,
And never notice, they're so asinine,
Asmodeus it is who eggs them on.
It's freedom that they fight for, each side says;　　　　2400
Look close, you see it's slaves that fight with slaves.
HOMUNCULUS. Never mind that men are so intractable!
They're all pitched out into the world; with tooth and nail
Each must defend himself as best he can—
That's the way a boy becomes a man.
But our problem here is how to cure
Our good friend Faustus lying prostrate there.
If you are able, go ahead and try;
If not, step back and leave his case to me.
MEPHISTO. I could try my Brocken dodges, but　　　　2410
Against me heathendom keeps its gate shut.
Those Greeks were never much, without the Bible—
All that naked, sensual razzle-dazzle,
That sinning with a light heart, gaily, freely!
Our sinning's serious, soul-torturing, gloomy.
So what's your plan?
HOMUNCULUS.　　　　　　Well, you were never shy
And if I say "Thessalian witches," I
Imagine you know what I mean.
MEPHISTO. [*Salaciously*]
Thessalian witches, my, oh my!
About them I have wondered a long time.　　　　2420
I doubt if it is lots of fun to pass
Night after night in their grim company,
But a short visit's worth a try, I guess.
HOMUNCULUS. Fetch the cloak and wrap our knight up in it!
The rag will bear you both, it's always done it.
I'll light the way.
WAGNER. [*Anxiously*] And me?
HOMUNCULUS.　　　　　　Hm, you.
Your place is here, you've still much work to do.

Unroll your parchments, diligently gather
The elements that the prescriptions call for
And mix them all together carefully;   2430
Think hard about the *what,* about the *how* still harder!
I meanwhile about the world will wander,
And maybe find the dot that dots the "i,"
And so at last complete the great endeavor.
Such great effort is rewarded worthily:
Wealth and fame, a long life and much honor,
Much knowledge and much virtue—possibly.
Goodbye!

WAGNER. [*Downcast*] Goodbye. Oh I feel sad, I do,
I fear this is the last I'll see of you.

MEPHISTO. Off, off! Peneios, here we come!   2440
My cousin here must not be underrated.
[*To the audience*] In the end we are dependent on
The very creatures we ourselves created.

CLASSICAL   WALPURGIS   NIGHT

BATTLEFIELD   OF   PHARSALIA

Darkness.

ERICHTHO. I am grim Erichtho, come once again,
As oftentimes before, to this horrid feast
Of ghosts. Don't think me so repulsive as
The wretched poets, slanderers all, delight
To paint me. Praising, blaming, it's no matter,
Their tongues clack on without a stop. —All along
The valley tents gleam whitely, like a pale sea,   2450
Shadows lingering still of that most harrowing,
Most cruel of nights. How often it returns,
The apparition, will return until
The end of time! Neither will let go
The empire to the other, and never to him
Who, having gotten it by force, by force
Maintains his rule. For men incapable

Of mastering themselves are all too ready
Masterfully to bend their neighbor's will
To their own. A great example's shown   2460
Us here: how force confronting greater force
And battling to the bitter end, freedom's
Lovely garland of bright flowers is torn
To bits and the stiff laurel's bent around
The conqueror's brow. Here Pompey dreamed how his
Triumphant youth had come again, there Caesar
Waked, watching with bated breath the wavering
Balance tongue. Strength against strength! And which
Prevailed, the world well knows.
                                           Campfires blaze,
Diffusing a red glow. The ground gives off   2470
The glimmer of blood spilt long ago, and all
The legions of Greek legend, tempted out
By the extraordinary brilliance of the night,
Foregather here. Fabled shapes from out
Of the olden days haunt half-glimpsed about
The fires, or sit beside them comfortably.
Still not at the full, yet radiant,
The moon swims up, shedding its mild light,
The phantom tents dissolve, the fires all
Burn blue. —But overhead, what's that   2480
Appearing unexpectedly, a meteor?
Its light shows up a round corporeal thing.
Ha, I smell life! No, it's not good, not right
To allow it near me, being as I am
A baneful influence on all that lives.
My reputation would decline still more,
To no good purpose. Down the meteor drops.
On due consideration, I withdraw.
                                                  Exit.

The Aeronauts Aloft.

HOMUNCULUS.
        I'll make a circle over these
        Ghastly fires once again;   2490

The valley bathed in silver haze
Presents a strange, a ghostly scene.

MEPHISTO.

It's like looking out the window
On my fearful Northern gloom,
Loathsome phantoms everywhere go,
I feel, I do, right at home.

HOMUNCULUS.

Look at that tall thing departing
With long strides, hastily.

MEPHISTO.

She looked up and saw us coming,
Thought, "This is no place for me."   2500

HOMUNCULUS.

Who cares? —Set your brave knight down
On the ground and in a breath
You'll see life return to him
Where he seeks it, in Greek myth.

FAUST. [*As he touches the ground*]

Where is she?

HOMUNCULUS.   I've no idea,
But this looks like a good place to inquire.
You might, before the dawn appears,
Scout around among these fires
And find what trace you can of her.
What should a fellow have to fear   2510
Who's dared to go down to the Mothers?

MEPHISTO. I have my reasons why I've come here, too.
So I suggest what's best for us to do
Is go our separate ways among the fires,
Each one seeking out his own adventures.
Then when it is time to reunite,
Little fellow, shine your tuneful light.

HOMUNCULUS. Like this I'll make it ring out, sparkle!
Off, off to many a new marvel!
[*The glass rings and lights up brightly.*]

FAUST. [*Alone*]

Where is she? —But never mind, don't fret. 2520
If this is not the very ground she walked on,
The wave that curled, breaking at her feet,
It's the air in which her Greek was spoken.
Here, miraculously, I'm in Greece!
Standing here, at once I knew the place.
Antaeus-like, life coursed again through me,
Dispelling all my languor with its warmth;
I'll search throughout this fiery labyrinth,
Encountering its fabulous company.

Exit.

ON THE UPPER PENEIOS

MEPHISTO. [*Snooping around*] Going around these fires I find I'm 2530
Ill at ease, it's all so strange, so foreign;
Stark naked almost all, they know no shame,
Only one or two have got a shirt on;
Immodest sphinxes, bold, unblushing griffins,
Things with wings and curling hair, queer demons
Presenting themselves front and rear to you!
It's true that au fond we're indecent, too,
But it's too natural, antiquity,
It needs to be redone in modern style,
Touched up with plaster into decency. 2540
Ugh, what people! Still, as a newcomer I'll
Behave as one should, greet all properly.
—Fair ladies, how d' you do, and how do y' do,
All you sage ancients, venerable gray ones!
GRIFFINS. [*Snarling*] Not gray ones, *griffins!* Mind what you say, will
you!
Who likes being called a doddering dodo?
Gray, grim, grouchy, grizzled, graveyard, gruesome,
All etymologically alike in origin,
Grate on our ear—we're not some grotesque relict.
MEPHISTO. Yet not to change this fascinating subject: 2550

You find *gr* a pleasing syllable
In griffin, your so honorable title.
GRIFFINS. [*Who never cease to snarl*]
Of course! You grab for gold, for crowns, for girls—
Griffin, grab, they're cognates, it's been proved,
Proof disputed often, but more often praised.
Who grip and gripe and grab, on them Dame Fortune smiles.
ANTS. [*A giant variety*] Gold, we heard. We've gathered lots, we have,
And stuck it all away in cliff and cave.
Those Arimaspians found out where it was
And stole it all away and laugh at us.   2560
GRIFFINS. Soon enough we'll force them to confess.
ARIMASPIANS. Not tonight you won't. Tonight we celebrate,
And by morning we'll have squandered it.
Ha, ha, this time we'll get away with it.
MEPHISTO. [*Having sat down among the Sphinxes*]
How nice it's here, at once I feel at home!
I understand you creatures, every one.
SPHINX. We utter our ghostly sighs and groans,
Then you lend your own sense to our sounds.
However—as a beginning, please, your name.
MEPHISTO. The names, the names inspired by my fame!   2570
—Are any English here? They love to tour around,
Survey old battlefields, view waterfalls
And dreary classical sites and crumbling walls—
This place would suit them right down to the ground.
They'd vouch for me: in an old British play
I have the part of "Old Iniquity."
SPHINX. And where'd they find that name?
MEPHISTO.   I've no idea.
SPHINX. Ah well. And stars, you understand their meaning?
What can you tell about the present hour?
MEPHISTO. [*Looking up*] I see shooting stars, a pale moon
          waning. . . .   2580
I like it here, it's such a cozy spot,
You warm me with your lovely lion's pelt.

A waste of time the stars, much rather I'd
Hear riddles or at least act a charade.
SPHINX. Say what you are, that's riddle enough for us,
Try, do, once, some self-analysis:
As needful to the pious as the wicked:
For the one a nimble duelist
To try their self-denying wards against,
For the other an ally in riot;   2590
And both, to Zeus, a comedy, a jest.
FIRST GRIFFIN. [*Snarling*] I don't like him.
SECOND GRIFFIN. [*Snarling louder*] Why's the fellow here?
BOTH TOGETHER. An ugly brute! Toss him out on his ear.
MEPHISTO. [*Savagely*] You think perhaps my nails can't do the
    damage
Your claws can? I'm ready for a scrimmage.
SPHINX. [*Mildly*] Stay, Sir, stay, don't get into a huff,
Soon enough you'll want to leave yourself.
At home, it may be, you cut quite a swath,
But here you don't feel right, is my belief.
MEPHISTO. You're very tempting upwards of your waist,   2600
But down below—oh horrible, a beast!
SPHINX. Rascal, you'll pay dear for your rude tongue.
Our claws are healthy ones and strong
And you with that weak, shriveled hoof of yours
Won't find it pleasant here, and with good cause.
        [*Sirens tuning up overhead.*]
MEPHISTO. What birds are those that I see swaying
In the poplars by the river?
SPHINX. Beware of them, their pretty singing
'S vanquished many a famous figure.
SIRENS.

    Ah, why linger, your taste spoiling,   2610
    With the ugly-fabulous?
    Hear the notes from our throats pouring,
    Sweet sounds and harmonious,
    As beseems our siren's voice.

SPHINXES. [*Mocking them to the same tune*]
    Make them come down from their perch in
    Those trees' lofty branches where
    They conceal their hawks' claws, sharp and
    Long as knives, with which to tear
    Limb from limb who lend them ear.

SIRENS.
    Let all hate and envy cease!   2620
    Stranger, listen to our offer
    Of such pleasure, happiness,
    As you'll nowhere else discover
    Underneath the skies of Greece.
    Find with us what joy, what peace!

MEPHISTO. That's the latest style of singing,
    Voice and string together jingling,
    One note through the other winding,
    I can do without such warbling.
    It titillates my ear to hear it,   2630
    But never reaches to the heart.

SPHINXES. Hear him—heart! Oh, but that's rich!
    A wrinkled, dried up leather pouch
    Better fits with that face, much!

FAUST. [*Appearing*]
    How wonderful this sight—repulsive creatures,
    Yet possessing powerful, grand features.
    It augurs well for me; oh I feel sure
    This solemn spectacle must lead somewhere.

FAUST. [*Turning to the Sphinxes*]
    Before these, fated Oedipus once stood.
    [*Turning to the Sirens*]
    Hearing these, Ulysses fought the hemp.   2640
    [*Turning to the Ants*]
    These gathered immense treasure in a heap,
    [*Turning to the Griffins*]
    And over it these faithfully kept guard.
    My soul's revived as if by a fresh breeze,
    How great these shapes, how great these memories!

MEPHISTO. I remember when you would have cursed
  The likes of these, and now they're to your taste.
  Oh but how a man is glad to have
  Even monsters help him to his love.
FAUST. [*To the Sphinxes*] You creatures shaped like women, answer:
  Where is Helen? Have you seen her?   2650
SPHINXES. She belongs to Greece's latter days,
  The last of us were killed by Hercules.
  Ask Chiron, he knows everything, he does;
  This haunted night he gallops up and down and back;
  If he stops to answer you, you are in luck.
SIRENS.
        Rather visit us, oh do it!
        Ulysses wasn't scornful, didn't
        Hurry past with eyes averted,
        Everything he knew he blurted
        Out to us, and we'd be glad to   2660
        Pass on all his news, all, to you.
        Only come down where we live by
        Green sea waters lapping softly.
SPHINX. That visit's one that we advise against!
  Ulysses had himself bound to the mast;
  You be bound, Sir, by us Sphinxes' counsel.
  Find noble Chiron if you're able,
  He'll tell you all you want to know
  Just as we have promised you.
                                        Faust departs.
MEPHISTO. [*Peevishly*] What's that I hear, those croaks, those
        whirring wings?   2670
  It all goes by too fast to see the things,
  One bird following another,
  They'd prove too much for any hunter.
SPHINX. It is the swift Stymphalides
  Who can outrun the winter's blast,
  The arrows of great Hercules
  Can scarcely reach them, they're so fast.
  They mean well, don't mind their croak.

With their goose feet and vulture's beak
They wish to demonstrate their kinship   2680
With us Sphinxes, win our friendship.
MEPHISTO. [*Pretending fear*] There's something in their midst that's
    hissing!
SPHINX. No need at all to fall into such terror,
    Those are the heads of the Lerneaen Hydra,
    Struck off the trunk, that you are hearing,
    And still they think that they are something.
    —But what's the matter anyway?
    You seem to want to get away.
    Well, go then! How you twist your neck
    To see that troupe there! Don't hold back   2690
    But introduce yourself at once,
    Enjoy a bit of dalliance
    With ladies of experience,
    The Lamiae! whose smiling lips and bold demeanor
    With all the Satyr race find favor.
    With Lamiae a goatfoot's able to
    Do everything that he's inclined to do.
MEPHISTO. But you'll stay here in case I should return?
SPHINX. Yes, yes! But go, the merrymakers wait.
    We hail from Egypt where we Sphinxes learn   2700
    To endure millennia on our stone seat.
    If you examine closely our position,
    You'll see we mark the months' and years' progression.
        Before the pyramids our stations,
        Witnessing the fate of nations,
        War and peace and floods go by,
        We watch all unblinkingly.

ON THE LOWER PENEIOS

Riverscape with Nymphs.

PENEIOS. Sedges, stir with a soft murmur!
    Sway, you reeds, and rushes whisper,

Rustle, yellow willow bushes,   2710
Sough, you trembling poplar branches!
Lull me back to peaceful dreaming—
A strange tremor in the ground
Wakes me with its anxious sound,
Wakes me from my quiet rippling.

FAUST. [*Coming to the riverbank*]
Unless I'm much mistaken, I
Hear, quite inexplicably,
Sounds I'd swear are human voices
Coming from these close-laced bushes.
The ripples seem to talk together,   2720
The breezes play tag with each other.

NYMPHS.

Sir, may we suggest
You lie down and rest
Beside the cool water
Where you may recover,
May find the repose
Your soul seldom knows?
We'll murmur, we'll whisper,
Till you sink in a drowse.

FAUST. *Now* I'm awake! How gladly I   2730
Surrender to the matchless forms
I've called forth here by my own eye!
How moved I am, amazingly!
What are they, memories or dreams?
Once, once before I knew such joy.
The water, sliding through the fresh,
Green-growing, swaying brake and bush,
Makes little noise, you hardly hear
A ripple; springs, a hundred, pour
From every side to come together   2740
In a pool whose pure, bright water
Doesn't frighten by its depth,
But makes a pleasant place to bathe.

Girls' limbs, in the liquid mirror
Glowing pink and white with health,
Delight the admiring eye twice over!
Bathing happily together,
Cautiously wading, boldly swimming,
At last, like schoolgirls, wildly screaming
They splash each other with the water.   2750
The pleasure this affords my eye
Should really be enough for me,
But still my mind keeps searching farther,
Would like to pierce that thicket yonder:
Its foliage, so rich and green,
Conceals the nymph who is their queen.

How wonderful! A fleet approaches,
Sailing in from the broad reaches,
Swans! Majestic, tender, calmly
Gliding side by side, yet proudly   2760
Turning head and beak—oh splendid
Creatures, haughty, self-delighted!
But one seems prouder than the rest,
Boldly puffing out his breast,
Sailing swiftly through his fellows
With his nobly swelling feathers;
Himself on white waves a white wave,
He swims straight to the sacred grove.
The others, plumage brightly gleaming,
Quietly are to- and fro-ing,   2770
Soon, however, make a rush at
All the flustered nymphs—they aim at
Making them forget their duty,
Only think of their own safety.

NYMPHS.
    Sisters, stoop and lay your ear
    To the river's grassy shore.
    Unless I am deceived I hear

Drumming hoofbeats heading here.
What messenger, I wonder, might
Be bringing news to us tonight?   2780
FAUST. The ground's ringing and the cause is
Hoofs, I think, a galloping horse's.
I search in the distance,
Can it be assistance?
Can I hope it's good fortune
He's bringing, that horseman?
And see, a rider's coming toward me,
As wise and brave a man as may be.
On a snow white horse he's mounted,
I recognize him, we're acquainted—   2790
Philyra's celebrated son!
Chiron, stop, I've got to speak to you.
CHIRON. Well, what is it?
FAUST.   Stop! How you keep on!
CHIRON. I *never* stop.
FAUST.   Then take me, please, with you.
CHIRON. Mount up and we will have a talk together.
Where to? You're standing on the riverbank;
I'll take you over, shall I, on my back?
FAUST. [*Mounting*]
Take me where you like, I'm in your debt forever.
—O you great man, O noble, lofty teacher,
Who trained a hero race, to his great glory,   2800
Brave Jason's Argonauts, that noble band,
And all who furnished poets with their epic story.
CHIRON. Forget that, please, I've put all that behind!
Even Pallas did herself small honor
By taking on the thankless role of Mentor.
In the end they do as they see fit,
Just as if they never had been taught.
FAUST. Profound physician, namer of all plants,
Best of all skilled in the lore of roots,
Who heals the sick and salves the wounded's smart,   2810

My arms embrace you here, so does my heart!
CHIRON. When a hero got hurt by my side,
    My science helped to mend his broken bones;
    But finally I put all that aside,
    Leaving it to priests and to old crones.
FAUST. You belong among the truly noble
    Who find all praise offensive, they can't bear it,
    Modestly they close their ears, won't hear it,
    Pretending there are others just as able.
CHIRON. A clever hypocrite you seem to be   2820
    Who flatters prince and people equally.
FAUST. Nevertheless I don't think you'll deny
    You knew the great and famous of your day
    And strove to emulate their finest deeds,
    To live as nobly as do the demigods.
    But which among the heroes of the past
    In your opinion were the greatest, best?
CHIRON. In Argo's glorious company
    Each hero shone in his own way,
    By his particular gift supplying   2830
    What in his comrades might be lacking.
    The Dioscuri led all others when
    Beauty was what counted, youth, élan;
    The two Boreads when a shipmate's peril
    Demanded the most resolute, quick action;
    Strong, reflective, wise, and patient in council,
    Jason, loved by women, was the captain;
    Then Orpheus: a gentle, pensive soul,
    Best of those who on the lyre played;
    And Lynceus, who steered night and day, sharp-eyed,   2840
    To bring the ship past jagged reef and shoal.
    Danger's best braved with your friends around you:
    Boldly you strike, and all your comrades cheer you.
FAUST. Nothing to say about great Hercules?
CHIRON. Don't speak that name, it wakes such memories!
    I'd never once seen Phoebus, Ares, or

Those others by whatever names they're called,
When big as life before me I beheld
The one men thought a god, so great their awe.
A king, a born king, Hercules, he stood there,   2850
Glorious-looking in his youth,
Submissive to his elder brother,
To pretty women, too, I fear.
His match you'll never see upon this earth,
Nor Hebe lead another upwards like him.
Vainly verse attempts, tongue-tied, to sing him,
Sculptors torture marble all in vain.

FAUST. They boast of their work, every one;
How short it falls of your description.
You've portrayed the fairest man,   2860
Now portray the fairest woman.

CHIRON. Ha, female beauty, what a bore—
So often statuelike, cold, stiff;
I reserve my praises for
Beings brimming with glad life.
The Beautiful delights itself,
To itself it's all in all,
But charm is irresistible,
Like Helen when I carried her.

FAUST. You carried her?

CHIRON.   I did, for sure.   2870

FAUST. Already I've been staggered, dazed—
And now I learn where she sat I sit, too!

CHIRON. She clutched my mane just as you do.

FAUST. Beside myself I am, half crazed!
Helen is my heart's desire.
Where was this, where did you take her?

CHIRON. Your question is soon satisfied.
Once it happened brigands seized her,
Then the Dioscuri freed her;
The raiders, unused to defeat,   2880
Rallying, rushed in hot pursuit.

I and Helen with her brothers
Raced along but found our course
Barred by the Eleusinian marsh;
The Dioscuri waded, I splashed over.
She, when we were safe, sprang down,
Sweetly stroked my dripping mane
And said such things, so charmingly!
So young she was, yet self-possessed,
Thanking me with such ease, grace—   2890
The joy it gave to an old man like me.

FAUST. And only ten years old!

CHIRON.   You've been taken
In, as I can see, by the professors,
Who've taken in themselves. Women
In mythology enjoy a special grace:
The poet shows them as his tale requires,
They never need endure a wrinkled face,
They keep their slim, attractive figures;
Carried off in youth—by crowds of suitors
Still pursued in age. In short: 2900
The calendar means nothing to the poet.

FAUST. Then why impose it on great Zeus's daughter?
On Pherae didn't slain Achilles find her,
Defying time's decree? Oh rare good luck,
From destiny's hard grip to snatch love back!
Why shouldn't I, with my fierce longing filled,
Bring back to life that form unparalleled,
That creature, goddesslike undying,
As dear as great, sublime as charming?
You saw her once, today I saw her, too,   2910
As fair, as longed for, as so long ago!
Her beauty's taken my whole being captive,
I'll make her mine, without her I can't—won't—live!

CHIRON. Your rapture, you strange fellow, is all too human,
But to us spirits you look like a madman.
Now as it happens you're in luck today:
I briefly visit Manto annually,

Manto, Aesculapius's daughter,
Who prays her reverend parent fervently
That he may, for the sake of his own honor,   2920
Teach physicians wisdom finally
And save the people from their reckless slaughter.
Of all the Sibyls she's best, I prefer her,
She's not some grotesque crone who raves and shrieks,
But kind and gentle, busy with good works.
Remain with her awhile, I feel assured
That with her herbs you'll be completely cured.
FAUST. Keep your cures, my mind's in perfect order—
She'd make me like the rest, ignoble, vulgar.
CHIRON. We've reached the healing well—now quick, alight,   2930
And drink its waters while you have the chance.
FAUST. Where have you carried me this dreadful night,
Splashing through pebbled streams? What place is this?
CHIRON. Here Rome's republic warred with mighty Greece,
Olympus to the left, Peneios right.
The greatest realm the world had ever seen,
Overthrown and swallowed by the sand,
The king in flight, the citizen exulting.
Look up and see, so close at hand,
The moonlit temple, still enduring.   2940
MANTO. [*Dreaming within*]
    Clattering hoofs
    Sound on the steps:
    Two demigods here.
CHIRON.
    Yes, yes—you are wise!
    Now open your eyes.
MANTO. [*Waking*] Hello! I see you've not failed to appear.
CHIRON. And I see that your temple is still here.
MANTO. You still race around, you're never weary?
CHIRON. You love best your quiet sanctuary;
    I love best to circle round the country.   2950
MANTO. It's time that circles around me—I wait.
    —Who's this?

CHIRON.   The tides of this notorious night
Have swept him here. The man's a lunatic,
Wants Helen and he wants her quick,
But hasn't got the least idea
How he should look for her or where.
He needs some Aesculapian therapy.
MANTO. I love the man who longs for what can't be.
                    [*Chiron is already far away.*]
Foolhardy fellow, enter and rejoice!
This passage follows a descending course   2960
Into Olympus's hollow foot, and there
Proserpine covertly cocks an ear
To hear an intruding footfall, living voice.
I smuggled Orpheus down there this way once;
So boldly does it, don't you spoil *your* chance!

A G A I N   O N   T H E   U P P E R   P E N E O I S

SIRENS. Dive into Peneios river!
Splash and swim, enjoy its sports!
Sing one song and then another
For these poor unfortunates.
Life on land is harsh and grim!   2970
If all of us went down together
To the green Aegean's brim,
What delights ours, every pleasure!

                                        [*Earthquake!*]

Water, backwards driven, surges,
Cast out of its ancient bed
In astonished, reverse flood,
Smoke pours from the cracked shore's fissures.
Quick, away all, never linger,
This does no one good, this wonder!

Noble guests, come too, come all,   2980
Join our gay sea festival
Where the tremulous waves sigh

Along the shingled shore and die,
Where Luna shines with double glow
And bathes us in her sacred dew!
There life's unconfined, and here
Earthquakes make one shake with fear.
If you're wise, away you'll hurry,
Here in this place it's too scary.

SEISMOS. [*Rumbling noisily down below*]
Once more, boys, a great big effort!   2990
All the strength you have, now use it!
When we break through, see how they will
Stare amazed and run off, fearful.

SPHINXES. What a dreadful trembling, shaking,
What a panic's in the air!
How all things are lurching, rocking
This way, that way—a nightmare!
It's too much, the whole affair!
But we won't stir from our place
Even if all Hell breaks loose.   3000

Now the ground thrusts up, in form
Marvelously like a dome,
And I know who's doing it:
It's the same Old One who built
Delos island to give shelter
To Latona, then in labor—
Pushed it up out of the waves!
How he lifts with all his might,
Muscles straining, great back bent
Atlaslike, and shoves and heaves   3010
Green riverbank and pebbly bed,
Gravel, earth, and grass and reed
Upwards, making a great gap in
Our peaceful valley region.
By his efforts unexhausted,
A colossal caryatid;

Buried still up to his waist,
He holds up the huge weight
Of granite, marble, quartz, and schist.
But no more, here he must stop,   3020
Sphinxes don't budge, not a step.

SEISMOS. All this is thanks to me, my doing,
Which in the end you must concede;
Without my shaking and my shoving
This world, this lovely world, how should
It ever have become so fair?
Your mountains towering in the air,
Into the pure and glorious blue,
Affording picturesque views to you—
Because of my drive, push, they're there.   3030

Under the ancient eyes of Night
And Chaos, pertly showing off,
I with the Titans threw about
Mount Pelion and Ossa both
Like two balls; in this way
We roughhoused in the joy of youth,
Till growing tired finally,
Wickedly giggling, clapped the peaks
Atop Parnassus—now he wears two caps.
You'll find Apollo up there, he amuses   3040
Himself with the blithe and buxom Muses.
I even raised aloft Jove's seat,
From where he wields his thunderbolt.
And now once more, prodigiously,
From below I've forced my way
And loudly summon dwellers here
To fill these slopes with life and cheer.

SPHINXES. We'd swear these mountains were primeval
If our own eyes hadn't witnessed
How they rose, a great upheaval,   3050

Bursting through the planet's hard crust.
A forest over it is spreading,
More cliffs appear, together jostling,
But we Sphinxes pay it all no heed:
Our seat's sacred, not to be disturbed.

GRIFFINS. Gold in all forms, leaf and nugget,
Glitter in the cracks of granite.
Ants, arise, they're thieves about!
With your fingers pick it out.

CHORUS OF ANTS.
After the giants'   3060
Great work is complete,
Up we go, we ants,
On our restless feet,
Darting in, darting out
Of the crevices where
Every grain we discover
Adds its little bit
Of worth to the treasure.
We search every corner,
Don't dawdle or slacken,   3070
Bring only pure gold in,
Ignore
The crude ore.

GRIFFINS. Heap it up here, all of it!
We'll squat down, our claws on it,
Good strong bolts they are, none better
For keeping safe the greatest treasure.

PYGMIES. It's really true, we've found a home!
How it happened? —no idea.
Never ask where we came from,   3080
It's enough that we are here.
All lands, great and small, provide
Life a place where it may thrive;
Where a cranny shows, be sure

Soon you'll see us dwarfs appear.
Man and wife together, we
Work in pairs exemplary
Of untiring industry.
Was Paradise like this? —can't say.
But here in this place we feel blessed   3090
And thank our stars, we're more than grateful.
Everywhere you look, east, west,
Mother Earth is kind, is fruitful.

DACTYLS.

If she in one night
Made these little ones,
She'll also beget
The littlest ones
Who looking round find
Lots more of their kind.

PYGMY ELDERS.

Move along, never stop,   3100
Occupy this fine spot!
Speed makes up for muscle,
So let's see you hustle.
It's peace still, get busy
And build us a smithy
To furnish our army
With weapons aplenty!

You ants, show you're useful,
Swarm about and discover
What we must have, metal.   3110
And Dactyls, so tiny,
Past counting, so many,
Your orders are:
Fetch fagots here!
Slow-burning fires will
Give us our charcoal.

GENERALISSIMO.

Go, valiant bowmen,
March out together,
Shoot the white heron
Nesting there, yonder,   3120
On that pond's shore,
Puffed with hauteur!
With one quick shot
Bring down the lot,
So every gnome
May flaunt his plume.

ANTS AND DACTYLS.

Who, who will save us?
We smelted the iron
And they, they did what, then?
Forged chains to enslave us.   3130
Rebel we will, but
It's too soon for that,
So stoop in submission.

THE CRANES OF IBYCUS.

Murderous shrieks and deathly moans!
Frightened flapping of white wings!
Dreadful cries of agony
Rise up to us in the sky!
All, all slaughtered, once so proud,
The lake crimson with their blood!
Greedy monsters without mercy   3140
Rob the herons of their glory;
Now plumes nod upon the helmets
Of those fat, bowlegged midgets!
You fellow cranes in your great V's
Flying above the heaving seas,
All together, come, we'll rally,
Assemble an avenging army!
We are kin, hear our appeal

In a cause concerns us all.
None must spare himself, we'll serve   3150
These ugly brutes as they deserve!

[*They fly off in all directions, croaking.*]

MEPHISTO. [*Down in the plain*] I know how to handle Northern
        witches,
    But these foreign ones give me the twitches.
    The Blocksberg region's such a pleasant place,
    No matter where, it shows a friendly face.
    Frau Ilse watches from her clifftop home,
    Heinrich high up smiles down amiably;
    The Schnarzers sneer at Elend, certainly,
    Yet everything stays put till kingdom come.
    But here! Go where you will, you never know   3160
    When there will be an eruption from below.
    Upon a valley floor I saunter blithely
    And suddenly there rises up behind me
    A mountain—well, a hill at least, let's say—
    That's more than big enough to bar the way
    To my dear Sphinxes. —Fires still burn brightly
    Lighting up the lurid scene around me,
    Revealing that pert troupe of flirts, still dancing
    Towards me teasingly, then with a mocking
    Laugh escaping. Careful! When you've stolen   3170
    Slyly in to snatch up sweets too often,
    You push at any door you think is open.
LAMIAE. [*Drawing Mephistopheles after them*]
        Go fast, then slow down,
        Hesitate, then race on!
        Linger to chatter
        Then off like birds, scatter!
        What fine entertainment,
        To make the old sinner
        Come hobbling after,
        Come stumbling hot for   3180

His favorite pleasure,
So as to find what?
A well-earned chastisement.
He drags his clubfoot,
As we flutter before him,
Slower and slower.
MEPHISTO. [*Coming to a stop*]
Damn, oh damn! Poor johnnies all,
From Adam on led to our fall!
A man gets old—but wise? Mooncalf,
Haven't you been fooled enough?   3190

The truth's well known, they're worthless through and through.
Rouged faces, bodies in tight corsets squeezed,
There's nothing good they have to offer you,
Take hold of them, you find their flesh diseased.
We understand it well, we see it plain,
And yet we jig when these jades call the tune.
LAMIAE. [*Halting*] Slow down, he's stopped, he hesitates, thinks
        twice.
Go back, or it's all over with the farce!
MEPHISTO. [*Going on again*] Keep going, don't get in a tangle
Of silly doubts! For who the devil   3200
'D be the Devil for a moment
If bewitching witches weren't?
LAMIAE. [*At their most alluring*]
Come, around our hero dance,
Love, we feel sure, will announce
Itself in him for one of us.
MEPHISTO. I'll admit in this uncertain
Light you look like pretty women,
So I will disparage no one.
EMPUSA. [*Pushing herself forward*]
Nor me neither! So I hope you'll
Let me join your friendly circle.   3210
LAMIAE. Always hanging round, she seems,

Spoiling all of our good times.
EMPUSA. [*To Mephistopheles*]
    We're related! I'm Empusa,
    A darling donkey-footed specter!
    Your foot's a horse's, still, dear cousin,
    I'll not refuse you a kind welcome.
MEPHISTO. I thought I didn't know a soul here,
    And find that we are all relations.
    An old, old story I see we are,
    From Harz to Hellas, all, all cousins.   3220
EMPUSA. I act fast and in a flash
    Assume whatever shape I wish.
    But in your honor I am glad
    To wear my long-eared ass's head.
MEPHISTO. Kinship here means much, I see—
    Such emphasis on family!
    But I'm not one who acquiesces
    In being linked to silly asses.
LAMIAE. Forget that hag, disgusting, ugly,
    She drives away all charm and beauty,   3230
    Wherever charm and beauty are,
    Let her appear and they're no more.
MEPHISTO. These other cousins, tender, luscious,
    Nevertheless make me suspicious;
    Those cheeks of theirs, blooming like roses—
    Behind them I fear metamorphoses.
LAMIAE. Try, though! You can choose from many—
    Courage! And if you are lucky
    You'll walk away with the grand prize.
    What good are all your amorous sighs?   3240
    For all your airs, your sneering, proud face,
    As a suitor you're a sad case!
    —Good, good, now he's joined the dance.
    Let your masks drop, show the dunce
    What you girls are really like.
MEPHISTO. The prettiest is the one I pick.

[*Embracing her.*]
Damn it, dry as a broomstick!
[*Grabbing another.*]
How about her? —That face, hard grin!
LAMIAE. You're owed better? Think again.
MEPHISTO. This one's petite. Let's bargain, dear.   3250
—A lizard, slips away so quick,
Her braid smooth and serpentlike.
Well, I'll take the tall one there.
—A thryrsus, that's what's in my grip,
With a pinecone on its top!
Where will it end? Look, there's a fat one,
Perhaps it's possible with that one.
Here goes with a last attempt!
She's flabby, doughy: in the East
Such creatures fetch the highest price.   3260
—But ugh! the puffball bursts apart!
LAMIAE. Scatter every which way, flashing
Bat-winged, silent, like black lightning!
In wavering, scary circles, each
Flap around that spawn of a witch,
Round and round the intruder swoop!
He is getting off too cheap.
MEPHISTO. [*Giving himself a shake*]
I never seem to learn, apparently;
It's stupid in the North, it's just as stupid here.
Here as there the ghosts are creepy, queer,   3270
The people crude, the poets equally.
Here as everywhere a masquerade
Sets your pulses going till your head
Is in a whirl. I see a charming masquer,
Pursue her and catch something makes me shudder.
Being fooled is just fine if
Only it lasts long enough.
[*Wandering among the rocks.*]
I'm lost. Where once there was a path

Is now a waste of stone and cliff.
I clamber up and down, halloo,   3280
"My good Sphinxes, where are you?"
Hopelessly along I stumble,
Finding no way through the rubble.
It's mad, it's crazy, just imagine,
In one night to raise a mountain!
That's a Witches' Ride, I reckon—
To pack along with them their Brocken!

OREAD. [*Out of the natural rock*]
Climb up here, my mountain's old as
Time, and keeps its ancient slopes,
Its venerable, granite steeps,   3290
The farthest-reaching spurs of Pindus.
Unshaken I stand as I did
When over me Pompeius fled.
But that illusion there, false show,
Will vanish at the first cockcrow.
I've often seen such spectacles put on,
Hold the stage awhile, then poof, they're gone.

MEPHISTO. Honor to you, you reverend peak,
With your great forests of stout oak,
Whose umbrage Luna's brightest light   3300
Strives in vain to penetrate!
—But in those bushes there I see
A spark glowing modestly.
How luckily things work out, yes,
It's him, it's him, Homunculus!
And where have you been, minikin?

HOMUNCULUS. Here and there and out and in,
Full of longing and impatience
To smash my glass, enjoy a real existence.
It's only that so far I've not met up with   3310
Any body I'd like to join up with.
However—let me say, between us,
I've been following two famous

Men, philosophers the pair are,
Whose every word is "Nature! Nature!"
I'll stick to them, I will, like glue;
The living world is surely what they know.
Everything they say I'll listen to
And learn from them the wisest way to go.
MEPHISTO. Go your own way, using your own mind!   3320
Where phantoms flourish, there you'll find
Philosophers, they're always welcome,
For they create new phantoms by the dozen.
Don't make mistakes and you will never learn!
You'd like to live, would you, be really born?
Well, you yourself must do that, on your own.
HOMUNCULUS. Still, good advice is not to be sneered at.
MEPHISTO. Well, go and we shall see how far you get.
                                    [*They separate.*]
ANAXAGORAS. [*To Thales*]
Your mind's stubborn, unrelenting.
What more proof, tell me, is wanting?   3330
THALES. The wave before the breeze runs glad enough,
But back from the precipice it flings itself.
ANAXAGORAS. Fiery gases gave this mountain birth.
THALES. In wetness lies the origin of life.
HOMUNCULUS. [*Between the two*]
Let me go along with you!
I yearn for a beginning, too.
ANAXAGORAS. In one night, my good Thales, did
You ever raise a mountain out of mud?
THALES. Nature's living stream never flows jerkily
By nights and days and hours, it runs steadily;   3340
She shapes all things by rule, isn't prone to quirks,
Force she abhors, even in hugest works.
ANAXAGORAS. She does, does she! Raging Plutonic fires,
The enormous explosive force of Aeolian vapors—
These broke through the old, flat crust of earth
And in a minute brought this mountain forth.

THALES. Yes, yes, it's there all right, fine, good—however,
　　A mere intrusion in the stream of Nature.
　　But it's a waste of time, such argument,
　　For those with patience enough to follow it. 　　　　3350
ANAXAGORAS. How fast the mountain fills with myrmidons
　　Who find a home in all the cracks and fissures,
　　Swarming pygmies, insects, and Tom-thumbs
　　And every kind of busy little creatures.
　　　　　　　　[*To Homunculus*]
　　You've never wanted power and dominion,
　　You've been a recluse, living in seclusion,
　　But if you're ready to take charge and govern,
　　I'll have you crowned as king of this great mountain.
HOMUNCULUS. And your opinion, my good Thales?
THALES. 　　　　　　　　　　　　　　　　Don't!
　　When you live with little people, 　　　　　　3360
　　The things you do perforce are little;
　　Among the great a little man grows great.
　　Look up and learn! See that black cloud
　　Descending on the pygmy nation,
　　Throwing them into confusion—
　　Cranes! and they, believe me, would
　　Destroy the king of Pygmies, too.
　　With sharp beaks, murderous talons,
　　Down they swoop on those felons
　　Like thunderbolts out of the blue. 　　　　　　3370
　　A crime it was to kill the herons
　　Stepping round their peaceful lake.
　　But those arrows which rained down
　　Murder on the innocent flock
　　Grew a bloody crop: in turn
　　The cranes, their rage excited by
　　Their poor kindred's tragedy,
　　Make pygmy blood pour out and soak the fields.
　　What good now their helmets, spears, and shields?
　　What good now his plume to every dwarf? 　　　3380

How the ants and Dactyls scurry off!
The pygmy legions waver, break, and fly.
ANAXAGORAS. [*After a pause, solemnly*]
Till now I've praised the powers underneath,
In this case I direct my gaze on high.
—Eternal Lady, ageless and unchanged,
Triple-shaped and triple-named,
My people perish! Hear me, hear me,
Luna, Dian, Hecate!
Soul-inspiring, pensive, most serious,
Calm appearing, fiery-amorous,   3390
Unclose your shadow's dread abyss,
Unconjured, bring down an eclipse!
                    [*A pause.*]
    How quick it's heard, my prayer!
    Has my loud cry
    Into the sky
    Disturbed great Nature's order?
The goddess's round throne swells larger
As it nears, burns whiter, brighter,
A monstrous, frightening light whose blaze
Purplish glows in blinded eyes!   3400
—No nearer, huge and menacing sphere,
Or you'll destroy us, us and all things here!

It's true, then, that Thessalian sorceresses,
Resorting to their wicked practices,
Once sang you down out of your monthly course
And wrung from you by necromantic force
Destructive powers? —Now the disc's turned dark,
It breaks apart and rains down burning rock
With such a clatter, noise of hissing flames,
Mixed with thunder, roar of hurricanes!   3410
Submissively I bow before the throne!
Forgive me, I called this disaster down.
                    [*Falls on his face.*]

THALES. The wonders this man thinks he heard and saw!
　　What happened I am not exactly sure,
　　But his ideas and mine are nowhere near.
　　We'll agree: the times are very queer,
　　But Luna still rocks high up in her sphere
　　Quite comfortably, just as she did before.
HOMUNCULUS. Look up to where the Pygmies made their home:
　　The mountaintop, once round, now's a sharp peak!　　　3420
　　I felt a huge, a cataclysmic shock
　　Caused by a boulder fallen from the moon.
　　Down it dropped, no questions asked,
　　And friend and foe alike were crushed.
　　Still, I must praise the skill, the might,
　　Able in a single night,
　　Working high up and down under,
　　To raise this mountain's mighty structure.
THALES. Don't excite yourself, it wasn't real.
　　That nasty brood are gone, and a good thing.　　　3430
　　Just imagine if you'd been their king!
　　And now let's off to the sea festival.
　　They're glad when strangers come and treat them well.
　　　　　　　　　　　　　　　　　　　　　[*They leave.*]
MEPHISTO. [*On the other side of the mountain, climbing*]
　　Look at me—scrambling up steep rocks,
　　Tripping over roots of wretched oaks!
　　In my dear pine-clad mountains of the Harz
　　There's a pitchlike smell, a smell I favor
　　Most of all, except the smell of sulfur.
　　But here among these Greeks there's not a trace
　　Of anything like that. I'm curious　　　3440
　　To find out what they use below in their Hell
　　To stoke the fires with, their kind of fuel.
DRYAD. I guess you're smart enough in your own country,
　　Abroad you're something less than apt;
　　Stop thinking home thoughts, try, Sir, to adapt
　　And show due honor to our sacred oak tree.

MEPHISTO. What you have lost, that's what you think about,
    What you were used to, that seems Paradise.
    —But what's that in the cave there my eye spies,
    Those three shapes squatting in the feeble light? 3450
DRYAD. The Phorkyads. Why don't you go inside
    And speak to them—unless you are afraid.
MEPHISTO. Well, why not? —I can't believe my eyes!
    I've been around, I have, yet must confess
    Nothing, nothing have I seen like these!
    The mandrakes take a back seat to such ugliness.
    The worst, most primal sins that ever were,
    When once you've laid eyes on this triple horror,
    Will seem quite innocent, demure.
    In our most dreadful hells we'd never suffer 3460
    Their even coming near the door.
    And here they're fixtures in the land of beauty,
    Antiquity's great home, as it's called proudly.
    They sense my presence, stir upon their seats,
    Squeak and twitter like vampire bats.
PHORKYAD. Hand me the eye, my dear, and I will
    See who's ventured near our temple.
MEPHISTO. Esteemed ladies, have I your permission
    To come and ask your triple benediction?
    You don't know me, that can't be disputed, 3470
    Yet I believe we're distantly related.
    I've seen a lot of ancient gods already,
    Bowed down to Ops and Rhea reverently;
    The Parcae, like you Chaos-born, I saw
    Just yesterday, or was it—I'm not sure.
    But your like till now's been denied to me.
    I'm overjoyed! That's all I have to say.
PHORKYADS. He seems to have some sense, that specter there does.
MEPHISTO. I'm so surprised no poet's hymned your praises.
    How has it happened, too, that I have never 3480
    Beheld your dignities portrayed in sculpture?
    It's you the chisel should attempt to capture,

Not Juno, Pallas, Venus, or whoever.
PHORKYADS. Sunk as we are in solitude and night,
  The truth is, we have given it no thought.
MEPHISTO. Of course not! You've been much too long concealed
  From the admiring eyes of the great world.
  You should be living in those places where
  Art and splendor, gloriously joined,
  Sit high upon a pedestal enthroned,   3490
  Where every day, turned out with record speed,
  A new marble hero lifts his sword,
  Where—
PHORKYADS. Enough! Don't waken wishes in us.
  What good, knowing such things, would it do us?—
  Born in the night, companions of the shades,
  Unknown to the world, hardly known to ourselves.
MEPHISTO. Never mind that, ladies. For your case,
  Hear what my suggestion is:
  Hand over one of you to someone else.
  With you three, one eye, one tooth suffice;   3500
  So shouldn't it be possible for you
  To squeeze together mythologically
  And as two instead of three make do?
  The extra shape you then could lend to me,
  Pro tem.
A PHORKYAD. Hm, hm—do we agree to it?
THE OTHERS. We do! Except the eye and tooth—they're out.
MEPHISTO. No, no, that's just what shows best in you women!
  To hit you off exactly, I must have them.
THE PHORKYAD. Keep one of your red eyes shut,
  Let a single fang stick out;   3510
  Seen in profile, then you would
  Look just like our sisterhood.
MEPHISTO. Agreed! I'm honored.
PHORKYADS.   Good!
MEPHISTO. [*A Phorkyad in profile*] So now it's done.
  Just look at me—Chaos's darling son!

PHORKYADS. And we his daughters—about *us* there's no doubt.
MEPHISTO. But dear me, when I think: the shame of it!
　　They'll jeer as I pass by, "Hermaphrodite!"
PHORKYADS. A new trio we are—beautiful!
　　Now we've two eyes, two fangs—wonderful!
MEPHISTO. With a face like this I'd better hide. I'll go　　　　3520
　　And scare the hell out of the devils down below.

ROCKY INLETS OF THE AEGEAN SEA

The moon arrested at the zenith.

SIRENS. [*Reclining on the rocks, playing flutes and singing*]
　　If Thessalian hags one night
　　Gave you such a dreadful fright,
　　Drawing you down wickedly
　　From your seat high up the sky,
　　Yet Dian, mild luminary,
　　We implore you, look benignly
　　Down upon these crisping wavelets
　　Scattering their silver droplets,
　　Shine upon the waters churning　　　　　　　　　　　　3530
　　With the crowds of creatures rising
　　From the waves, all at your service.
　　Queen of the Night, bright moon, be gracious!
NEREIDS AND TRITONS. [*Appearing as wonders of the deep*]
　　Sound a shriller note to call up
　　From the deep the scaly sea folk
　　Hiding in the depths below!
　　Down we dove, for shelter from
　　The howling chaos of the storm,
　　To the quiet bottom: now
　　Your sweet music draws us here!　　　　　　　　　　　3540
　　See with what delight we wear
　　Golden chains and rarest jewels,
　　Bracelets, buckles, silver girdles.
　　To your song we owe this treasure

Got from hulks upon the sea floor
Shipwrecked following your lure.
—O spirits of our rocky shore!
SIRENS. We know very well you fishes
Love your sea life, its salt freshness,
Where you dart about carefree.   3550
But upon this festive day
Demonstrate, for such our wish is,
That you're more than thoughtless fishes.
NEREIDS AND TRITONS. The selfsame thought was ours, too,
Before our coming here to you.
Sisters, brothers, off! We'll manage
It by means of a brief voyage:
Furnish proof conclusive that we
All are more than fishes only.

                                           [They depart.]
SIRENS. Off they go in a flash!   3560
Where to? Samothrace,
With the wind at their tail!
We wonder what object
They have for their visit
To that island where
The Cabiri, those queer,
Mighty deities dwell—
Gods who beget themselves
Solitarily from themselves
Over and over,   3570
Yet have no idea
In the least what they are.

Lovely Luna, graciously
Stay your passage through the sky,
Keep it midnight still, and thus
Dawn, detained, shan't scatter us.
THALES. [*On the shore, to Homunculus*]
I'd be glad to take you to old Nereus.

His cavern's close by, too, but that old walrus
Is so difficult, ill-tempered, sour,
Grumbles that he cannot find   3580
An ounce of good in humankind.
Yet he can see into the future,
For which he's held in general esteem;
And he's helped many, I'll say that for him.
HOMUNCULUS. So let's knock and see what happens. I'm
Not afraid for my glass, little flame.
NEREUS. I hear something—human voices, are they?
Instantly I'm thrown into a fury!
Ambitious creatures all, who try to be
Like the gods, yet doomed eternally   3590
To end at last just as they were at first.
I might have passed these years in godlike rest,
But felt impelled to shower all the best
With good advice and still more good advice.
And then I see what they do—wrong, all wrong!
I might as well have held my foolish tongue.
THALES. Yet, Old Man of the Sea, we've faith in you.
Your wisdom's famous, don't turn us away.
Regard this flame, seems human, it is true,
But it will do exactly as you say.   3600
NEREUS. As I say! They hear but never heed,
Shut their minds against my every word.
As often as they bitterly condemn
A thing they've done, they do the same again.
How like a father I warned Paris, often!
Don't, I said, seduce that foreign woman.
There he stood upon the Greek shore, boldly;
I told him what in vision I saw clearly:
The smoke-filled air, shot through with a red glow,
The roofs ablaze, murder and death below: 3610
Troy's judgment day, fixed in epic verses
Millennially, as terrible as famous.
An old man's words made that vain puppy smile;

Lust led him on, Troy's topless towers fell:
A giant corpse, stark after its long torture,
Providing Pindus's eagles a fine dinner.
Ulysses, too! Didn't I foretell him
Circe's tricks, the Cyclops' frightfulness,
His dillydallying, his shipmates' brainlessness,
And what else, heavens! What good did it do him?   3620
Till ten years overdue, half drowned, storm tossed,
A kind wave bore him to a friendly coast.

THALES. A wise head is distressed by such behavior;
A good heart tries again because it's good.
An ounce of thanks contents the kindly mentor,
Outweighs a ton of black ingratitude.
The boy here hasn't come to beg a trifle.
He wants to live! For that he needs your counsel.

NEREUS. Don't spoil it when for once I'm in good humor!
Quite other things are on my mind today.   3630
My children are expected, every daughter,
The lovely Dorids, Graces of the Sea.
Not high Olympus, no, not all your Greece
Shows figures suaver than my dears possess.
From water dragons gracefully they leap on
The white-maned horses of earth-shaking Neptune,
With the element they're so at home
They seem uplifted by the very foam.

Galatea, loveliest of all,
Borne on Aphrodite's scallop shell   3640
Sparkling opal-like, comes here today.
She, since the Cyprian forsook us—
Forsook her birthplace in the sea—
In Paphos now is worshiped as a goddess;
The temple city and the chariot throne,
The foam-born's once, are now my daughter's own.

Leave me! In a father's hour of pure bliss
There's no place in his heart for curses, bitterness.

Go ask that wonderworker, Proteus,
The way one's born or changed to something else. 3650
       [*Departs seaward.*]
THALES. We've not advanced a single step by this.
 If we catch Proteus he'll turn to water
 In our grasp. If he stays put, he'll mutter
 Such strange things to make our poor heads spin.
 Still, what you need's advice, the more the better,
 So it's worth trying. On our way, my son!
         [*They go off.*]
SIRENS. [*On the rocks above*]
 What's that we see approaching
 From far out in the offing,
 White sails, they look like, bellying
 In the brisk wind blowing.   3660
 How brightly round a light's shed—
 They're mermaids, but transfigured!
 Down, sisters, we'll go, shall we?
 Those are their voices surely.
NEREIDS AND TRITONS.
 You'll welcome with delight
 Whom we bring here tonight:
 Figures austere, still,
 Emerging shining from
 Chelone's giant shell—
 And gods all, every one!   3670
 Then sing and louder sing.
SIRENS.
 Tiny yet boasting great power,
 Ancient, revered deities,
 Snatching the shipwrecked sailor
 Out of the turbulent seas.
NEREIDS AND TRITONS.
 We bring you the Cabiri
 To rule this happy revel,
 Their presence, holy, peaceful,
 Calms Neptune so he's friendly.

SIRENS.

> We yield to divine power: 3680
> When ships are wrecked and helpless,
> With oh what strength, stupendous,
> You rescue the seafarer.

NEREIDS AND TRITONS.

> We've brought along three,
> The fourth wouldn't come;
> Claimed he, only he,
> Was the true, rightful one
> Who thought for them all—
> He refused our appeal.

SIRENS.

> One god ridicules another,   3690
> All are worthy of our honor.
> Praise their mercy, fear their anger!

NEREIDS AND TRITONS.

> They're seven, all told, really.

SIRENS.

> The other three, where are they?

NEREIDS AND TRITONS.

> We don't know, don't ask us,
> Inquire on Olympus.
> Also the eighth's there that
> Nobody's thought of yet.
> Benignant, all, to us but
> Unfinished still, imperfect.   3700
>
> None there are like these gods,
> Ever pressing onwards
> With hungriness unspeakable
> For the unattainable.

SIRENS.

> All, all the gods, wherever,
> In sun or moon or sky,
> We reverence in prayer:
> It pays, does piety.

NEREIDS AND TRITONS.
>Now, now's our finest hour—
>We lead this jubilee!   3710
SIRENS.
>The heroes of old story,
>The bravest men of Greece,
>Now see their fame grow dim.
>Their efforts won for them
>The winged ram's Golden Fleece,
>But yours, the great Cabiri!
>[*All together.*]

>But ${our \atop yours}$ } —the great Cabiri!

[*Nereids and Tritons pass off across the stage.*]

HOMUNCULUS. These misshapen things, they look
>Like old pots of clay.
>The learned break their heads to think   3720
>What they signify.
THALES. Yes, what's old they covet most:
>The coin is precious for its rust.
PROTEUS. [*Unobserved*] Old fabulist that I am, this delights me!
>The queerer something is, the more it suits me.
THALES. Where are you, Proteus?
PROTEUS. [*Throwing his voice, now sounding far off, now near*]
>   Right here! —and here!
THALES. I do forgive you your old jokes, dear fellow,
>But don't try fooling me, a friend, for you know
>You're able to sound far off when you are near.
PROTEUS. [*As if from far away*]
>Bye-bye!
THALES. [*Whispering to Homunculus*]
>   He's here, right here! Now sparkle, flash!   3730
>He's just as curious as a fish;
>No matter where he lurks or what his shape,
>A light will tease out the old scamp.
HOMUNCULUS. There, it's brighter now, the spark;

Any brighter and the glass would break.

PROTEUS. [*As a giant turtle*]

    What thing's giving out that pretty light?

THALES. [*Tucking Homunculus out of sight*]

    Good! —Come closer for a better look,

    But on two man's-legs, hear! The change won't put

    You to much trouble, I imagine—right?

    Who wants to see what I have hidden here   3740

    Needs our approval and consent, dear Sir.

PROTEUS. [*In noble human shape*]

    Still up to your old sophist's japes.

THALES. And you're still fond of switching shapes.

        [*He uncovers Homunculus.*]

PROTEUS. [*Astonished*] A dwarf that shines! That's something new for

    me.

THALES. He needs advice, he's anxious to be born.

    The dear thing came, as I've heard him explain,

    Into the world halfway, amazingly.

    He's all there mentally, he thinks all right,

    But bodily he's null. All the weight

    He's got is in the glass. He'd like to have   3750

    A tangible existence, really live.

PROTEUS. A true virgin birth, I see—

    He's here before he ought to be.

THALES. [*Lowering his voice*]

    That's not all that's not quite right.

    I think he's an hermaphrodite.

PROTEUS. All the better. He can go, whenever

    He gets a body, one way or the other,

    As the circumstances may require.

                  [*To Homunculus*]

    —But come, there's no need here for prolonged thought,

    The open sea is where you make your start.   3760

    You're small, so you begin on a small scale,

    Enjoy devouring what is smaller still,

    Till growing bit by bit you will arrive at

Higher stages, loftier forms of attainment.
HOMUNCULUS. The air's so soft here, with a breath
I simply love of wet, green growth.
PROTEUS. I believe you, dear boy that you are!
And farther out upon this narrow tongue
The misty sea air's even fragranter.
And look there, moving steadily along—   3770
It is the pageant coming into view.
Let's go see it.
THALES.   I'll come, too.
HOMUNCULUS. Extraordinary, our trinity:
Three spirits walking out in company!

[*Telchines of Rhodes on hippocamps and sea dragons, flourishing
Neptune's trident.*]

CHORUS OF TELCHINES. We forged the trident of Lord Neptune
By which he rules the boisterous ocean.
When black clouds with a loud uproar
Are let loose by the Thunderer
And lightning plummets down the sky,
Neptune flings up in reply   3780
Wave after wave defiantly,
And all things struggling fearfully
Between the two, worn out and battered,
By the deep are soon devoured.
Tonight, entrusted with his scepter, we
Can ride the waves without anxiety.
SIRENS.
Votaries of Helios, blessed
With days that know no rain or mist,
Greetings to you at this time
In which we honor midnight's queen.   3790
TELCHINES. Dear goddess beaming proudly from high up there,
How pleased you are to hear praise of your brother!
Then lean your ear toward blissful Rhodes, for there
Our endless paeans to him fill the air.

His fiery gaze looks down upon us when
His day's course is begun and when it's done.
We please him, our cities, mountains, bays,
And so he blesses us with his warm rays.
No fog descends on us, and if it should,
It's scattered by a sunbeam, puff of wind.   3800
Unnumbered statues give him back his likeness
As mild, sublime, as youth, as huge colossus.
We were the first to show divinity
In human form, nobly, worthily.

PROTEUS. Let them go on singing, bragging!
Those dead shapes, to the life-giving
Sacred sunlight, are a joke.
Untiringly those people work
At smelting bronze, and when it's cast:
See, a marvel! is their boast.   3810
But how does it end up with these
Grandiose god effigies?
Along a quake comes, knocks them flat,
And all that grandeur's sold for scrap.

All men do upon dry land
Is only labor without end,
The eternal sea suits life much better.
So off you go into the water
With your uncle Proteus,
Who changes to a dolphin—thus!   3820
            [*He transforms himself.*]
There, there's just the place for you,
Mount my back, I'll carry you,
To the ocean marry you.

THALES. The wish to start at the beginning
Of creation, is deserving
Of all praise. Be prepared
For working hard, at top speed.

Obedient to eternal laws,
Whirled through eons without pause,
Through more forms than head can reckon,   3830
You'll mount upwards till you're human.

[*Homunculus mounts the back of dolphin-Proteus.*]

PROTEUS. Bright spirit, come, we'll dive into the wet,
Although there's nothing much of you as yet.
There at last you'll live in three dimensions,
Free to move about in all directions.
But one caution: don't aspire
To mount the rungs of nature's ladder.
For once you reach the top, become
A man, that's it, you're finished, done.
THALES. Maybe so. Still, I'll defend a life   3840
Lived worthily in its brief time on earth.
PROTEUS. A life like yours, yes—it persists
Well past the bounds of mortal days.
Among the crowd of pale and drifting ghosts
I've noticed you these many centuries.
SIRENS. [*On the rocks*]
See, around the moon bright clouds
Make a shining ring, they're doves
Aglow with love, with wings as white
As the goddess's own light.
Paphos sent them here to us,   3850
Venus is their patroness:
Now our festival's complete,
All's pure joy, without a spot.
NEREUS. [*To Thales*]
For the nighttime wayfarer
The ring's a trick of light and air,
But we spirits stick to our opinion,
Never doubt it is the right one:
Doves they surely are, believe me,

Escort for my daughter's journey
On her shell. How they fly's   3860
A marvel, learnt in the first days.
THALES. Yes, a good man's simple faith
Is after all what's best, what's right:
A holy sense, nursed in the warmth
And silence of the inmost heart.
PSILLI AND MARSI. [*Riding sea bulls, sea calves, sea rams*]
In Cyprus's deep caves
Where Neptune's booming waves
Halt, foaming, at the sill,
Where Seismos cannot shake
The massive roofs of rock,   3870
Fanned by the eternal breeze,
With quiet pleasure still,
As in the eldest days,
We guard the Cyprian's shell—
In which, when night winds whisper,
Across wave-woven water
We bring our lovely mistress.
Unseen by the new race
Usurping this our place,
We go about our duties   3880
Undismayed, quite heedless
Of Eagle and Winged Lion,
Of Crucifix and Crescent:
Thrones transitory, restless,
Now rising up ascendant,
Now overthrown and fallen,
That drive out and that kill,
That lay waste town and field.
But we, now and forever,
Come bringing Galatea.   3890
SIRENS.
Now unhastily approaching,
Ring within ring smoothly turning

Round the chariot planetlike,
Or wound round it serpentlike,
Come the Nereids, stout figures,
Boisterous yet pleasing creatures,
Also Dorids, mere wisps, tender,
Bringing with them Galatea,
She who is most like her mother:
Olympian her gravity,   3900
Immortal and deservedly,
But so charming, too, and winsome
In the way of earthly women.

DORIDS. [*As a chorus, passing by Nereus astride dolphins*]
These blooming youths, Dian, illumine
With your beams of silver light
So our father may salute
The dear husbands we have chosen.

                    [*To Nereus*]
They are shipwrecked boys we rescued
From the clutch of the fierce surf
And on beds of moss and seaweed   3910
Warmed them back again to life,
Who now, proving true hearts, thank us,
As they should, with burning kisses.
Your favor, Father, them vouchsafe!

NEREUS. A double boon, deserving of applause:
You're merciful, and you enjoy yourselves.

DORIDS.
If we've done well, our father,
Do say yes to our request,
Say they may stay young forever,
Pressed to our immortal breast.   3920

NEREUS. Your lovely prizes, daughters, have,
Enjoy your youths and make them men,
But it's not my prerogative
To grant what only Lord Zeus can.
The waves by which you're rocked and tossed

Forbid love should, for you, endure,
And when your fancy fades at last,
Then gently put your youths ashore.

DORIDS.

You're very dear, sweet boys, to us
But part we must, can't help it;   3930
We wished for everfaithfulness,
The gods will not allow it.

THE YOUTHS.

Be as you've been, we'll not repine,
Brave sailor boys as we are,
We've never known so good a time,
We shouldn't want a better.

[*Galatea appears on her shell.*]

NEREUS. It's you, it's you, my darling daughter!
GALATEA. What happiness! My dear, dear father!
Stop, dolphins! I'm seized by the sight of him.
NEREUS. Past me already, they sweep on, spray flying,   3940
What do they care for the heart's inmost feeling?
How much I should like it to be with them!
But even a passing look's enough
To pay me for the long year's dearth.
THALES. Hurrah! Again hurrah! I feel
Such joy: the true, the beautiful
Possesses my entire being.
In water all has its beginning,
All life's sustained because of water,
Life-giving Ocean, rule forever!   3950
If the clouds didn't come, big with your moisture,
To pour rain down on the brook-laced pasture,
To fill the streams, in a wild race tumbling
Down to the rivers winding and turning—
For our mountains and plains, our earth, what should we do?
Over and over life's refreshed thanks to you!

ECHO. [*A chorus of all the voices*]
    Over and over fresh life pours up from you!
NEREUS. Swinging back, far out at sea,
    So far I can't make out my girl,
    In still wider circles they   3960
    Turn and turn, a gay display,
    To crown the water festival.
    Repeatedly I glimpse the shell
    Glittering like a star amid
    The sea-skimming multitude:
        She, she, so dear,
        Who though so far from me,
        Shines clear, shines near,
        Through all eternity.
HOMUNCULUS. In this delicious damp and wet   3970
    No matter where I shine my light
    All's simply so lovely.
PROTEUS. In this life-giving damp and wet
    Oh how your tiny, tinkling light
    Now rings out bright and bravely.
NEREUS. In the midst of the dolphin-riding host,
    What new mystery's being made manifest?
    What is it flames all round the shell, a bright jet
    Of fire that stoops at the goddess's feet,
    Now blazing up fiercely, now burning low,   3980
    Like a heart full of love beating fast, beating slow?
THALES. It's our little fellow, Homunculus,
    Incited, inspired by old Proteus!
    What you see are the signs of irresistible longing,
    And aren't those anguished sounds amorous groaning?
    He'll smash himself, he will, on her throne, wait and see.
    There! A flash, a bright flame, and he's spilt in the sea!
SIRENS. What marvel of brightness transfigures the water,
    The waves as they break shooting out sparks of fire?
    Such effulgence, such bursting and flashing of light,   3990

Every creature aflame as it swims through the night!
How sea, how shore's held in a burning embrace!
Then let Eros reign with whom all things commence!
 Hurrah for the ocean! Hurrah for the waves
 And their crests with the sacred fire ablaze!
 Hurrah for the water, hurrah for the fire,
 Hurrah for their union, so rare, with each other!
ALL TOGETHER. Hurrah for the soft, caressing breezes!
 Hurrah for the caves, all mysterious places!
 Lift up our voices in praise of the four: 4000
 Water, fire, earth, and air!

ACT III

BEFORE MENELAUS'S PALACE AT SPARTA

Enter Helen, with a Chorus of Trojan Women and Panthalis, the Chorus Leader.

HELEN. I am the much admired, much blamed Helen,
Come up from the beach where just now our ship landed
And giddy still from the tossing of the waves,
Which with Poseidon's blessing and Eurus's strong
Push, bore us on their bristling, high-arched
Backs from the Phrygian plain to our native shore.
Below King Menelaus and his veterans
Are busy celebrating their return.
But you, O great house of Tyndareus,   4010
Give me, your child once, welcome—house
My father built near the slope of Pallas's hill
Following his return, and fitted out
More splendidly than any in all Sparta,
In those dear days when I grew up here playing
Happily with my sister Clytemnestra,
With Castor and with Pollux, too. How glad
I am to give you greeting, great bronze doors!
Upon a festive day once, folded back
In welcome, a light shone through them, it was he,   4020
Was Menelaus, chosen out of many,
My bridegroom! Open, doors, once more
To me so I may do, as a wife should,
The urgent bidding of the King. Let
Me in! And let remain behind all
The calamities by which I've been besieged
Till now. For since the fateful day I stepped
Across this threshold, with no cares on my mind,

To worship at the shrine on Cythera,
As my duty was, but there to be seized by   4030
That ruffian, that Phrygian, so much
Has happened, things that people everywhere
Delight to tell, but no delight for me
To hear, whose story, longer with each telling,
Has grown into a legend, much mouthed tale.
CHORUS. O great Lady, never scorn that highest
Honor—fortune—gift which you and you
Alone have been allotted: beauty so
Sublime there's no renown compares with it.
The hero's name's heard long before he comes   4040
And so his step is proud. But let him be
The stubbornest man alive, before all-
Conquering beauty he'll humble his proud mind.
HELEN. Yes, yes. But with my husband by ship I
Arrived, here to his city have been sent
Ahead, and what he means by it I cannot
Guess. Am I here as his wife, the Queen?
Or am I to be sacrificed to appease
His royal hurt and the long-endured misfortunes
Of the Greeks? I'm a captive, am I too   4050
A prisoner? I've no idea. Oh but
It's true: for me the immortal gods decreed
A most equivocal fortune, equivocal fame,
The doubtful fellows of my handsomeness,
Who even now stand here beside me at
The door, lugubrious and threatening.
In the hollow ship my husband hardly looked
At me, nor spoke one word of reassurance.
He sat facing me and seemed like one
Who meditated evil. But once having   4060
Entered the bay into which Eurotas's waters
Pour, the lead ships' prows barely scraping
The beach, as if the god were prompting him,
He spoke: "My men will debark here, all in good order,

I'll muster the ranks on shore. But you go ahead,
Driving your horses along Eurotas's wet
And fertile bankside, flower-filled meadows, till
You come to Lacedaemon's lovely plain,
A broad and fruitful field once, surrounded
By frowning mountains. Enter the high-towered   4070
Palace, call the household staff together,
The shrewd old woman, too, I left in charge.
Let her show you all the store of wealth
Your father left, treasure I have kept
On adding to through years of war and peace.
You'll find, I'm sure, all's just as it should be,
For princes can expect, when they come home,
To find that nothing's not in its right place—
Servants aren't authorized to change things."
CHORUS. Your eyes rejoice, heart swell, Queen, at the sight   4080
Of all that treasure: wealth and still more wealth!
In there you'll find gold chains, gems, diadems
Glittering in their pride and vanity. Go in
And challenge them, their ranks are soon drawn up!
How much, how very much I'd love to see
Your beauty in a trial of arms with gold and pearls.
HELEN. And then my lord gave me a further charge:
"When you've completed a thorough, point by point
Inspection of the house and stores, collect
As many tripods as you think you'll need,   4090
Together with the other kinds of vessels
That the rites of sacrifice require: cauldrons,
Shallow basins, bowls; pour tall jugs full
Of purest water from the sacred spring;
Have ready wood that's dry and quick to catch;
And finally, be sure a sharp knife's there.
All else I leave to you." Those were his words
As he urged on my going. But no word, none,
What living, breathing thing he means to offer
Up to the Olympians. Oh, I am full   4100

Of such misgivings! But no, don't think of it.
All's as the gods dispose, who cause to happen
What they choose, let men think well or ill
Of it. We mortals, we must suffer what
We must. How often has the slaughterer,
Devoutly raising high the heavy ax
Above the tethered victim's drawn-down neck,
Found himself prevented by an enemy's
Appearance or the intervention of a god.

CHORUS. What's to come, no thinking can search out—   4110
Then, Queen, take heart and boldly go in there!
Good and evil come upon us un-
Predictably. And even when predicted,
Do we credit it? Troy, burning, fell,
Death stared us in the face, yet don't we stand
Here at your side your happy servants still,
The bright sun shining overhead, for our
Own mistress the brightest being here below.

HELEN. Well, come what may! In any case what I
Must do now, dawdling no more, is go up in   4120
The palace I've been parted from so long,
Missed so much, and almost forfeited
So foolishly. I can't believe it, there
It stands! These feet won't bear the woman
Up the steep steps as lightheartedly
They did the skipping child long years ago.

                                                                       Exit.

CHORUS. Sad captives though we are, come, sisters, put
All grief aside and share our lady's joy,
Share Helen's joy at coming back again
To her paternal house—coming back,   4130
It's true, belatedly, but for that very
Reason with a gladder heart, a firmer foot.

The gods, the holy gods, be praised to whom
Such happy homecomings are owed! The one
Who's been delivered from his chains, soars

As if on wings above what's harsh and hard,
While with his arms upstretched in hopeless longing
The captive pines behind his prison wall.

But her, so far off as she was, a god
Snatched up out of the rubble heap of Troy   4140
And brought back to her old home, new
Restored, where after pleasures, after sufferings
Defying all description, she'll recall
The dear days when she was a child.
PANTHALIS. Leave off your jubilation, sisters, look:
There at the bronze doors I see someone, can
It be the Queen? And hurrying back to us
Upset and pale? —Queen, what's the matter, what,
Inside the halls of your own house where you
Expected only smiles of welcome, has so   4150
Unsettled you? Don't try to hide the loathing
I see in your face, the indignation struggling
With surprise.
HELEN. [*Who has left the doors open behind her, very upset*]
            Zeus's daughter's not
A prey to common fears, I never feel
Chill-fingered panic's light, swift touch; but the horrors
Starting up out of the womb of ancient
Night in which things had their first beginning,
With shapes as many as the burning vapors
Billowing from a crater's fiery mouth,
Make even heroes' hearts turn faint. When I   4160
Went in the house, the infernal gods in
Just such fashion made their presence known,
So that my only thought was, leave, yes, gladly
Leave, with back turned on the threshold so
Familiar once and so much longed for since.
But no! I've fallen back, afraid, into
The light, but farther back than this, O you
Grim powers, howsoever called, you'll never
Drive me! I'll take care to purify

The house so that it's fit to welcome to   4170
Its bright hearthside its Lady and its Lord.
CHORUS LEADER. Tell us, Mistress, us your servants who
    Stand by you always, what thing happened there?
HELEN. What I've seen, your own eyes shall see,
    Unless Old Night's already swallowed her
    Grim creature back into her womb. But let
    Me try as best I can to put it into
    Words: When I walked with solemn steps
    Into the royal house's dim interior,
    My mind intent on what I must do first,   4180
    I found to my surprise that all was emptiness
    And silence: no sound of hurrying feet along
    The corridors, no servants running back
    And forth about their work. And no one, maid
    Or old housekeeper, came to greet the stranger
    In the customary way. However, as I
    Neared the hearth I saw, by the dying embers'
    Glow, a muffled figure seated on
    The floor: a woman, tall, and looking more
    Like someone lost in thought than napping. "Up,"   4190
    I ordered her, "go back to work at once"—
    Thinking she must be the one my husband
    Left to keep the palace when he sailed
    Away. But still she sat there, huddled up,
    Not stirring. I warned her she must rise. At last,
    As if to motion me out of the house, she lifted
    Her right arm. Furious, I turned
    Away and hurried toward the steps that led
    Up to the richly furnished sleeping chamber,
    With the treasure vault close by. The monstrous figure 4200
    Sprang up from the floor; peremptorily
    It barred my way, a tall, gaunt shape with hollow,
    Bloodshot eyes, a shape to make your senses
    Swim, head whirl. Oh, it's a waste of breath,
    Impossible, to try with words to show a figure
    To the life. —But there she is herself!

And bold enough to venture out into
The light! Yet we're the masters here until
The King arrives. Apollo, lover of things
Beautiful, stops these horrors in their tracks   4210
Or sends them scurrying back into their holes.

[*Phorkyas appears at the threshold.*]

CHORUS.

So much I've lived through, although bright ringlets
Wave like a young girl's all round my temples,
Much that was dreadful, past all describing:
War's awful anguish, Troy in the night
Of its fall.

Out of the dust clouds, uproar of soldiers
Hand-to-hand battling, fearfully I heard
Ear-piercing gods' shouts, heard frightful war-strife's
Brazen voice drawing near and more near   4220
To the walls.

Oh, still high aloft Ilium's
Walls stood, but the devouring flames
Raced from neighbor to neighbor house
Setting roof after roof ablaze,
With their hot-blowing breath they raged
Over the night-shrouded city.

Running, I could see, dim through the murk
And the flickering fire's glare,
Full of wrath, the dread gods approach,   4230
Giant figures of wonder
Striding on through the gloom of the
Billowing, crimson-tinged smoke clouds.

Or did I see them? Terrified,
Maybe I imagined it all?
But who can say, I shall never be

Sure. Yet I know for a fact,
What I see now, this horrible
Creature, I see. If I were
Not so afraid, I even could   4240
Touch the hag, seize the witch with these
Hands of mine—but I dare not.

—Which of the daughters
Are you of Phorkys?
You've got the look of
One of those creatures.
Are you perhaps one of the Graiae,
Born ancient and gray-haired,
With between you one eye, one tooth,
Which you pass round as needed?   4250

Horror, how dare you
Venture where beauty is,
Show your disgusting face
Under Apollo's
Critical eye? But it's no matter—
What is ugly he never sees,
As his heaven's eye never,
Looking down, sees a shadow.

Mortals, however, such is their
Hard lot, have to endure the un-   4260
Speakable pain that all lovers of
Beauty must feel when their eyes are afflicted by
What is vile and forever cursed.

Yes, so listen sharp: dare to be
Smart with us, and I promise you
The dreadfullest menaces, awfullest curses
You've ever heard, pouring out of the mouths
Of us lucky ones formed by the gods.

PHORKYAS. The saying's old and still as true as ever:
  Modesty and beauty never walk   4270
  The green earth side by side, hand clasping hand.
  Their ancient loathing for each other is
  So deep-rooted that if their paths should
  Cross, right around they turn and rush
  Apart as fast as legs can carry them,
  Modesty dispirited, beauty
  Insolent as always till she passes
  Down into the Stygian dark, unless
  Old age has tamed her first. You make me think,
  You cheeky, foreign things, hussies from   4280
  Across the sea, of screeching cranes that fly
  Past overhead, like a trailing cloud, so clamorously
  The quiet wayfarer lifts his head to look;
  But they keep on their way, he keeps on his,
  And that's how it will be with us. —Who are
  You anyway to raise a racket here
  Before the palace of the King, like raving
  Maenads or a bunch of drunken women?
  How dare you howl at me, the housekeeper,
  Like dogs that bay the moon? Do you   4290
  Imagine I don't know what sort you are,
  Spawned in war and nursed in battle? Itching
  After men, seduced and then seducing,
  Sapping soldiers' strength, and citizens'
  Too! A locust plague you look like, gathered
  Here, that swarms down on the ripening crops
  And eats up others' industry, lays waste
  What grew, before you came, so prosperously!
  Base captured goods, for sale or for exchange!
HELEN. Scolding servants in the presence of their mistress   4300
  Is grossly to infringe on her authority.
  It's her business, no one else's, to praise
  Those who deserve praise, punish the remiss.
  Moreover I'm content with how they served

Me when great Ilium was besieged, and fell,
And lay stretched out; and with their conduct
Too during all the ups and downs, the hardships
Of our wanderings, a time when one
Was apt to think of oneself first. And I
Expect the same good service from my cheerful   4310
Women now we are in Sparta. The master's
Not concerned with who his servants are
But with how well they serve. So hold your tongue,
And no more of those grinning looks at them,
You hear? If you have taken good care
Of the household in the mistress's absence, you've earned
Her praise. But now she's here herself. Return
To your old place, or your reward will be,
Not thanks for doing well but some smart slaps.

PHORKYAS. It's her right, yes, our heaven-blessed Lord and
      Master's   4320
Spouse, to chastise servant girls; she earned
It by long years of prudent management.
I recognize you now, our Queen and Mistress;
And since you have returned to occupy
Your old position, take the reins, do, slack
So long, into your hands, take full charge
Of the house, its treasure, all of us. But please:
First of all protect me from this pack,
Who next to you, a very swan for beauty,
Are no more than noisy barnyard geese.   4330

CHORUS LEADER. How ugly next to beauty ugliness is!
PHORKYAS. How stupid next to good sense stupidness is!

[*From here on members of the chorus step forward singly to speak.*]

FIRST CHORIST. Do tell us of Father Erebus, Mother Night!
PHORKYAS. And Cousin Scylla, what do you hear from her?
SECOND CHORIST. The monsters, oh dear me, that swing in your
      family tree.
PHORKYAS. Take a trip down to Hades, visit your relatives there.

THIRD CHORIST. The people who live there are much too young,
  much, for you.
PHORKYAS. There's ancient Tiresias, go and make love to him.
FOURTH CHORIST. Orion's nurse was your great-great-grandchild.
PHORKYAS. The Harpies had your care and feeding, right?   4340
FIFTH CHORIST. What *do* you eat to keep your scrawny shape?
PHORKYAS. Never the blood that you're so greedy for.
SIXTH CHORIST. You hunger for corpses, yourself a revolting corpse.
PHORKYAS. Vampire's teeth shine in your nasty mouth.
CHORUS LEADER. I could shut yours if I said who you are.
PHORKYAS. Name yourself, too, and both secrets are out.
HELEN. It makes me sad, not angry, to have to inter-
  Vene to stop this violent bickering.
  Nothing damages the good order of a household
  More than a feud that festers underneath   4350
  The surface among its master's faithful servants.
  His commands do not harmoniously
  Echo back to him in the form of promptly
  Executed work; no, all is jarring
  Discord, self-will; in the confusion he
  Himself's confused and scolds away to no
  Avail. And that's not all. In your discourteous
  Rage you've conjured up before me such
  Unhappy visions, horrid, crowding shapes
  That pluck at me so that I feel I'm being   4360
  Dragged, in spite of standing here on my
  Own native ground, down to Orcus. Are
  These memories? Or is it some delusion
  Gripping me? Was I that person? Am
  I still her now? And shall be in the future—
  The sweet dream and the nightmare of those wasters
  Of proud cities? My girls tremble; you,
  However, an old woman, are unmoved.
  Make sense, will you, of all this for me!
PHORKYAS. If one looks back on long years of good fortune,   4370
  The extraordinary favor of the gods

Comes at last to seem a dream. You
Were blessed beyond all measure in your life—hero
After hero hot to have you, ready
For no matter what foolhardy under-
Taking. Avid with desire, Theseus seized
You young, a man as strong as Heracles,
With such a splendid figure, too.

HELEN. Carried me, a ten-year-old, slim
As a doe, off to Attica, where Aphidnus   4380
Kept me for him in his citadel.

PHORKYAS. But soon enough set free by Castor and by
Pollux, after which a host of heroes,
All outstanding men, came courting you.

HELEN. But the one I favored secretly, I must
Confess, was Patroclus, Pelides' second self.

PHORKYAS. But father wanted Menelaus, bold
Sea rover, also careful landlord.

HELEN. Yes, gave him me; the rule, too, of his realm.
And from our union sprang Hermione.   4390

PHORKYAS. But when he was contesting an inheritance
In far-off Crete, and you were left alone,
A much-too-handsome visitor appeared.

HELEN. Don't remind me, please, of my half-widow-
Hood and all the terrible disasters
That were its bitter consequence for me.

PHORKYAS. That trip of his cost me my Cretan freedom:
A captive, slavery was my hard fate.

HELEN. He sent you here at once to manage things
For him, his palace, boldly gotten wealth.   4400

PHORKYAS. Which you forsook, eyes fixed on many-towered
Ilium, love's inexhaustible delights.

HELEN. Delights! Endless sufferings, bitter more
Than words can say, were heaped upon my head.

PHORKYAS. But what they say is, two of you were seen,
One in Ilium, also one in Egypt.

HELEN. Don't addle my poor addled wits still more!
Even now I don't know who I am.

PHORKYAS. They also say Achilles rose up from
  The empty shadow world, on fire still,   4410
  To love you as he had done once before,
  In defiance of the strict decree of fate.
HELEN. I married him, a phantom to a phantom!
  It was a dream, as "phantom" itself says.
  I'm fading, feel a phantom once again. . . .

[*She falls into the arms of the half chorus.*]

CHORUS.
        Quiet, quiet, you evil-eyed, serpent-tongued hag!
        From such monstrous single-toothed chops, such a hideous
          gullet,
        What but foul things are breathed! Malevolence wearing
        A face wreathed in smiles, a ravenous wolf in sheep's
          clothing,
        Is more to be feared than the three-headed dog's jaws.   4420
        We wait here and wonder, afraid: when and where where
          will it strike,
        This lurking monster of malice crouched in the dark?

        When what's needed are kind words consoling the sore
          heart, assuaging
        Lethean words, out of the past you malignly rouse up
        Not the good, no, the worst things and instantly all's
          plunged in gloom,
        The present's bright face, the future's first faint gleam of
          hope.

        Quiet, quiet, so the soul of Queen Helen, momently
        Ready to flee, shan't lose hold of, let go of
        The loveliest form that the sun, shining down, ever's seen.

[*Helen, recovering, again stands amid the women.*]

PHORKYAS. Come out from the clouds, golden sun of our day,   4430
  Who delighted us veiled and now dazzles our sight!
  How the world unfolds for you yourself's able to see.

I'm ugly, they say, yet know beauty's bright face.

HELEN. I'm still all atremble from fainting away,
How weary my bones are, how I long for repose!
But a Queen must be ready, as indeed all men must,
To meet every danger that's waiting to pounce.

PHORKYAS. You stand there before us, so lovely, sublime,
Your look is commanding, command what you wish.

HELEN. Redeem the lost time your rude quarreling cost!   4440
Get ready the sacrifice our King decreed.

PHORKYAS. All's ready, the tripod, the bowl, and sharp ax,
The water, the incense, but the victim? —please say.

HELEN. The King gave no hint.

PHORKYAS.   Gave no hint? Woe is me!

HELEN. Woe? What do you mean?

PHORKYAS.   Queen, it's you who is meant.

HELEN. Me?

PHORKYAS. Yes, and these here.

CHORUS.   Oh what horror!

PHORKYAS.   The ax
Is for you.

HELEN.   I foresaw it, I did!

PHORKYAS.   And I see
No way out.

CHORUS.   And ourselves?

PHORKYAS.   *She* will die as a Queen.
But hung from the rooftree like thrushes just snared,
You'll dance in a row, your feet kicking the air.   4450

[*Helen and the Chorus freeze in an attitude of astonishment and*
terror.]

PHORKYAS. You're ghosts, all ghosts! Yet there you stand like creatures
Turned to stone, in dread of being banished
From the day, that's not for you. It's just
The same with men: all ghosts like you, and like
You loath to quit the glorious sunlit world,
But no one's here to plead for, rescue them.

All know, few like, the end that always waits.
Enough! You're finished, done for. Now to work!

[*Claps her hands. Masked dwarfs appear at the door and swiftly do as they are commanded.*]

Come on, you sad-faced, paunchy freaks of nature!
Waddle over here, here's mischief to be done,   4460
All that your hearts desire! The altar, gilt-horned,
Set down in its place; the shining ax,
Lay it along the silver edge! Fill up
The water jugs: to wash away the gruesome
Black bloodstains! Now spread the costly
Carpet on the ground so that the victim
May kneel royally and then, wrapped up
In it, be buried fittingly, without
Delay, though with her head cut off.
CHORUS LEADER. The Queen's walked off to one side, thinking,   4470
The girls are wilting like mown meadow grass.
I'm the eldest, have a solemn duty,
As I think, to talk about all this
With you, who are so very, very old.
You've seen a lot, you're wise and seem to mean
Us well, in spite of the mistaken, brainless
Way these women acted toward you. Tell
Me then if you know how we might be saved.
PHORKYAS. Indeed I do. If the Queen will save herself,
She can, with you thrown in—it's up to her   4480
Alone. But resolution's called for, speed.
CHORUS. Honored most of the three Parcae, wisest of the Sibyls, you,
Don't unsheath the golden scissors, keep us here in light and life!
We can feel our legs already dangling, twitching in the air,
Legs we'd much prefer to dance with, sinking breathless
    afterwards
On our lovers' breasts.
HELEN. They're terrified. Well, I am not, it's pain
And sorrow that I feel. But if you know

Some way to rescue us, how grateful we
Should be. A circumspect, shrewd head   4490
Is able to see possibilities where none
Seem to exist. Say what you have in mind.
CHORUS. Tell us, yes, oh tell us quickly how we can escape the noose
    Which, just like a dreadful necklace, they'll draw tight around
      our throats!
    We can feel our life already, breath stopped, passing out of us,
    If you, Rhea, the gods' mother, turn your face away from us,
    Wretched us!
PHORKYAS. What I propose requires a long prologue—
    Have you the patience to listen quietly?
CHORUS. Lots, oh lots! To listen is to live.   4500
PHORKYAS. The prince that stays at home and guards his wealth,
    Keeps his palace walls well mortared, sees
    To it the roof keeps out the driving rain,
    He'll prosper all the days of his long life.
    But let him rush off somewhere irresponsibly,
    Impiously deserting house and hall,
    And he may find the old place still there, coming
    Back, but changed, how changed, if not in ruins.
HELEN. What's the point of this familiar wisdom?
    Say what you have to say, but keep away   4510
    From subjects I find painful in the extreme.
PHORKYAS. I'm recounting past events, mean no
    Reproach. Menelaus coursed the sea,
    From bay to bay he went in search of plunder,
    Raiding islands and along the seaboard, bringing
    Booty back, great heaps of it, that's stored
    Inside the palace. Ten long years he spent
    Before the walls of Troy; how long it also
    Took him to come home I do not know.
    But his great house, how is it with it now?   4520
    With all of Sparta?
HELEN.   Finding fault again!
    Is it so much your nature you can't speak
    Without an accusation tumbling out?

PHORKYAS. The highlands in the north, in back of which
　　The Taygetos ascends, have been forgotten
　　All these years—it's from there Eurotas
　　Starts out as a lively brook, and dropping
　　Down the valley broadens out into the reed-
　　Lined stream that feeds your swans. In that hill country
　　Back there a bold race, appearing out　　　　　　　　4530
　　Of the Cimmerian dark, have settled down and built
　　A stronghold none can scale, from where they harry
　　The whole countryside just as they please.
HELEN. They did all that? It seems impossible.
PHORKYAS. They had the time, it must be twenty years.
HELEN. Have they a chief? Are they a band of brigands?
PHORKYAS. No, they're not. And yes, they have a chief.
　　He raided here once but I don't complain.
　　He could have taken all we have but only
　　Chose a few things—gifts, he said, not tribute.　　　　4540
HELEN. How did he look to you?
PHORKYAS.　　　　　　　　Not bad at all!
　　I liked him—cheerful, lots of spirit, a fine figure
　　Of a man, and sensible as few Greeks are.
　　They're called barbarians, those people, but
　　I doubt there's one of them as savage, bloodthirsty,
　　As many a hero showed in front of Troy.
　　I'd trust myself to him, his magnanimity.
　　And you should see his castle! Not at all
　　The heap of clumsy stones your fathers, Cyclops-
　　Fashion, piling block upon unmortared　　　　　　　4550
　　Block, haphazardly threw up. There all
　　The verticals are plumb, the horizontals
　　True. Before your eyes it soars into
　　The sky, a close-joined structure, steely smooth.
　　To scale those walls—the thought itself slides helplessly
　　Back! And inside, oh what spacious courtyards!
　　All around which buildings stand of every
　　Kind and purpose, with pillars, arches low
　　And lofty, balconies, and galleries

4560

That give upon the outside and the in.
And there are coats-of-arms.

CHORUS. Coats of what?

PHORKYAS. You saw how Ajax had a coiled snake
On his shield. The Seven against Thebes each bore
A rich device on his shield, too, with its
Own meaning: moon and stars in the night sky;
Goddesses and heroes; ladders, swords
And torches and whatever else with which fine cities
Are threatened and besieged. These heroes, too,
Bear such devices, brightly colored, going
Back to the remotest times: lions, eagles, 4570
Beaks and claws, buffalo horns, roses,
Peacock tails; and also bands of gold
And black and silver, blue and red. They hang
In long rows in great halls that stretch
Away into the shadows endlessly—
What dancing you'd have there!

CHORUS. And dancers, do
They have them?

PHORKYAS. Yes, the best! Golden-haired
And lively footed, breathing sweet youth
Just as Paris breathed it once when he
Approached too near to Helen.

HELEN. Keep, please, to 4580
The story you were telling!—finish it.

PHORKYAS. *You* finish it—by saying clearly, in a firm
Voice, yes! Upon which I will set you safely
Down inside that castle.

CHORUS. Say it, yes,
One little word, and save us all!

HELEN. What, should
I fear the King would overstep the bounds
So far as to do me harm?

PHORKYAS. Do you forget
The unheard-of cruelty with which he butchered

Fallen Paris's brother, your dear Deiphobus,
Who recklessly grabbed up the widow—you—   4590
For his blissful concubine? He sliced his nose
And ears off, Menelaus did, as well
As other parts—oh, it was horrible.
HELEN. Because of me he did that, yes.
PHORKYAS.   Because
Of him he'll do the same to you. Beauty's
Not divisible; who's possessed her for
His own is not about to share her out.
He'd sooner kill her, cursing less than all.

[*Trumpets sound in the distance, the Chorus shrinks in fear.*]

As cruelly as the trumpets pierce your ear and grip
Your bowels with anguish, just so jealousy's   4600
Sharp claws grip his heart: he can't forget
What once was his and isn't any more.
CHORUS. Don't you hear the bugles blowing, see the flashing of bright
     arms?
PHORKYAS. Welcome, Lord and Master, I will gladly render my
     account!
CHORUS. And us?
PHORKYAS.   You know already. Her death first,
     Then yours, inside. There is no help for it.
                                                         [*Pause.*]
HELEN. My mind's made up, I know what I must do.
     An evil spirit I'm afraid you are,
     Who turns what's good into its opposite.
     All the same I'll do it, go with you.   4610
     And afterwards? That's as it may be, what
     The Queen's thoughts are is locked inside her bosom,
     And may it stay so. —Woman, lead the way!
CHORUS. How glad we are to go, and just as fast
     As legs can carry us! Death close behind,
     But looming up before us a great stronghold
     With walls unbreachable—oh may it keep

Us just as safe as Ilium's did, which only
A low trick was able to bring down.

[*A mist springs up, gradually obscuring the scene.*]

But what, I wonder, 's going on, what's happened   4620
To the sun? Oh sisters, look, the plumes
Of mist which waver up from Eurotas's holy flood
And quite blot out its lovely, rush-crowned banks!
And where are they, the swans, the free, the proud,
Who so delight to glide together up
And down the stream?—they're nowhere to be seen.

But listen! That's their hoarse song sounding
Far off, it foretells, it's said, their death.
Please let it not be heralding, instead
Of our deliverance, our death, too, so swanlike   4630
As we are with our long, lovely curving
Necks and snowy throats—or heavens, hers,
The swan-begotten! Woe, no end of woe!

All's lost in mist now, ourselves as well.
Whatever's going on? I can't tell
If we are treading ground or air, so light
Of foot we seem. Do you see anything?
Can that be Hermes hovering in front, that gleam
His golden staff commanding our return
To gray, unpleasant Hades—Hades always   4640
Packed to overflowing with weightless shapes,
And always empty, silent, desolate?

All at once the mist disperses, nothing sunny, bright revealing,
Only stone gray, brick brown walls that stare down blankly all
        around us,
Bringing up short the eye's freedom. It's a courtyard? Or a cavern?
It's no matter, it's so awful! Oh dear sisters, it's a prison,
We are captives more than ever!

COURTYARD OF A CASTLE

Surrounded by ornate, fantastic medieval buildings.

CHORUS LEADER. Just like women, to jump so to conclusions!
  Slaves of the moment, the weather, every turn
  In our fortunes: whether good, whether bad, neither   4650
  Is calmly endured. One of you always
  Contradicting the other and being contradicted in turn;
  When joy makes you exult, pain howl and weep,
  It's only then you sing in unison.
  Now quiet down and wait to hear what our
  Mistress shall decide, for herself and us.
HELEN. Where are you, Pythoness, if that's your name?
  Come out from inside this castle's vaulted gloom!
  Perhaps you went to tell that wonderful,
  Heroic lord of yours that I am here   4660
  So he may welcome us. If that's the case,
  My thanks, now take me in to him at once!
  I've wandered long enough, it's rest I want.
CHORUS LEADER. It's no use, Queen, your peering all about,
  The ugly creature's vanished. Maybe she
  Is still there in the mist that we emerged
  From so abruptly, who knows how, for no one
  Stirred a limb. Or maybe she is wandering
  About the labyrinthine halls of this
  Strange place, which looks like several castles huddled   4670
  Into one, to find its lord so he
  May come to give you greeting. —Yes, see there,
  Above: already there are servants bustling
  All about the galleries, windows, doorways.
  It shows a great reception's being prepared.
CHORUS. Oh, look over there, it makes my heart leap!
  Lovely boys in procession descending the stairs
  With so wellbred a manner, ceremonious tread,
  Not a one out of step! Who's the person arranged
  This and did it so soon? What is most to admire   4680

In these good-looking boys? Their lightness of foot?
Or the blond locks that curl round their radiant brows?
Or downy cheeks blushing, like peaches, in pairs?
I'd be tempted to bite one, but shrink back in fear,
Remembering how, in a similar case—
How disgusting the thought is!—eager mouths chewed,
Instead of ripe fruit, bitter ashes.
    But here the dears come,
    And what's that they have?
    A carpet, a throne,   4690
    Steps to mount it,
    A fine-broidered canopy!
    Billowing softly,
    It's drawn, like a heaven
    Of garlanded clouds,
    Over our Queen's head.
    For, begged to be seated,
    She has taken her place
    In the sumptuous chair.
    —Women, advance,   4700
    Range yourselves silently
    Row on row, on the steps.
    Fitting, yes, fitting, entirely fitting,
    I gratefully say it, her welcome here is!

[*The Chorus's words accompany the action on the stage. When the
last of the long line of pages and squires have arrived below, Faust
appears at the head of the stairs, dressed like a medieval courtier, and
descends with dignified, slow steps.*]

CHORUS LEADER. Unless the gods, as they so often do,
    Have lent this man his handsome figure, noble
    Bearing, affable air for a brief moment
    Only, everything he undertakes
    Must end in triumph, over soldiers in grim
    Battle or pretty ladies in the little wars   4710
    Of love. I like him better, I do, yes,
    Than many a much-admired one these eyes

Have seen. And look, the Prince approaches, with a slow
And reverential step. Queen, turn your head!
FAUST. [*Advancing, with a man in chains beside him*]
Instead of welcoming you with proper ceremony,
With the reverence that you are owed, I bring
You this man bound in chains: failing in his duty,
He made me fail in mine. Down, fellow, on
Your knees, confess your guilt before the queen
Of women! A man with eyes extraordinarily   4720
Keen, his post was in the tower, to scan
The sky and earth for anything that showed
Itself between the valley's boundary
Of hills and our castle here: moving herds
Upon the plain, perhaps, or armed men
On the march—protect the one, we do,
The other we confront. But today, what
A fiasco! You arrive and up above all's mute,
Which makes us fail to greet so eminent
A guest with all the honors due her. By   4730
His negligence he's forfeited his life
And already would have met the bloody end
He well deserves, except it's you alone
Shall punish or shall pardon, as you will.
HELEN. How high a dignity I am allowed—
To be the judge, the ruler here, though it
Should only be (for so I must suppose)
By way of a probation. Very well, then, as
The judge my first duty is to give
The accused a hearing. Prisoner, speak!   4740
LYNCEUS THE WATCHMAN.
Let me kneel, look at her, careless
Whether life or death await me—
To this woman Heaven's sent us
What devotion's mine already!

Watching for the light of morning
Eastwards, where its pale path lies,

Miraculously, without warning,
Southwards the sun seemed to rise!

Turning that way, what I see is
Neither high hill nor steep canyon,   4750
Neither heaven's, earth's expanses,
Only her, unrivaled woman.

Mine are eyes that see as sharply
As a lynx's, hence my name,
Yet I found that all around me
Seemed a dark and cloudy dream.

I was lost, could make out nothing,
Neither towers, parapets;
Then the mist abruptly lifting,
Forth a golden goddess steps!   4760

Dazzled, I could only stand there
Drinking in the glorious view;
As her beauty blinds us all here,
So, wretch, I was blinded, too.

I forgot my watchman's duty,
Unblown hung my horn this morning—
Menace me with death, do! Beauty
Makes all threats seem hollow, nothing.
HELEN. I may not punish wrongdoing I'm the cause
Of. What an unrelenting fate pursues me,   4770
To turn men's heads so violently that they
Are heedless of themselves, of honor, every-
Thing. They ravish, they seduce, fight wars, run here,
Run there. Both gods and heroes, demigods and even
Evil spirits have dragged me all around,
I don't know where. When I was simply one,
The turmoil that I caused; more turmoil still
When there were two of me; now I am three,

Am four, trouble after trouble, endlessly.
This man is blameless, set him free! He's not   4780
Disgraced, the man a god has driven mad.
FAUST. I look in wonder, Queen, at her who shoots
Unerringly, at him who's shot. I see
The bow that sped the arrow, the man brought down
By it. Still you let fly, and who's the mark
Now?—me! In court and castle, all about
Me, there's the swish of feathered shafts. What am
I now, who once was lord and master here?
My staunchest troops you make forget their duty,
My walls a doubtful shield. I fear it's you   4790
My army will obey, all-conquering,
Never conquered Lady, you! There's nothing
I can do but yield myself and all
That I in my delusion thought were mine.
Freely now I kneel before you, loyally
Acknowledge you my Queen, who soon as she
Appeared, my throne and all I own were hers!
LYNCEUS. [*With a chest, followed by men carrying more chests*]
I'm here again, Queen, I've come back—
A rich man, see, who begs a look!
He looks at you and feels at once   4800
A beggarman and a rich prince.

The man I once was, am I now?
What's there for me to wish for, do?
It's no use now my piercing sight,
Back it's beaten by your light.

Out of the East we came, a host,
And it was all up with the West;
So vast a multitude we were,
The van knew nothing of the rear.

The first line broke, the second held,   4810
The third came on with sword and shield;

Behind each man a hundred waited,
The thousands slaughtered went unheeded.

We drove ahead and conquered all,
Imposing as we went our rule,
And where I gave the orders Sunday,
Another robbed and stole on Monday.

We looked for booty on the run,
Grabbed up the prettiest girls, each one,
Grabbed up the fattest, best livestock,   4820
And every horse there was we took.

But I, what's priceless I looked for,
For things extraordinary, rare;
What others seized on as a prize
Was dust, was dry straw in my eyes.

The treasure in deep caves concealed
My sharp vision soon revealed;
No pocket but I saw into it,
No chest so stout but I saw through it.

Great heaps of gold coin I now own   4830
And every kind of precious stone;
The emerald's celestial green
Is only fit for your breast, Queen.

Now let this pearl fetched from the floor
Of ocean, dangle from your ear!
Red rubies, paling, scared, must yield
Before your blushing cheeks the field.

So riches beyond all compare
I bring the one who is most fair,
And set them humbly at your feet,   4840
The spoils of many a bloody fight.

As many chests as I have brought,
As many iron ones I've got;
Admit me to your company,
I'll stuff with gold your treasury.

No sooner do you mount the throne
Than reason, wealth, the royal crown,
Surrendering their powers, stoop
Before your unexampled shape.

All, all that I rejoiced was mine   4850
Is gone from me, is now your own,
The things I thought most rare, most precious,
I now see they are nothing, worthless.

No rich man am I any more,
What's wealth, it's only dust and straw.
Oh, give it back by one glad glance
The worth that was its proud boast once!
FAUST. This precious freight obtained so bravely—off
    With it! No, I don't reprimand you, but
    I shan't reward you either. Everything   4860
    The castle holds is hers already, offering
    Her now this, now that, is meaningless.
    Dispose these riches no one's seen as yet
    To best effect; make a glorious display
    Of them. The vaults above our heads make sparkle
    Like the heavens, with lifeless things persuade
    Her it's a living paradise she's in!
    Go on ahead to lay down carpets flowered
    Like the spring. Let her feet tread only
    On what's soft as lawn, her eyes see splendor   4870
    That would strike blind all but gods.
LYNCEUS.
    It's little enough what you, Sir, ask,
    A pleasure for me, not a task.
    Gladly wealth and blood, knees bent,

Submit to beauty's government.
Our swaggering soldiers meekly stand
With blunted sword and nerveless hand.
Let her appear, even the sun
Suffers by comparison;
The rich garden of her face   4880
Makes all else seem a desert place.

HELEN. [*To Faust*] I'd like to speak to you—but come up here
Beside me, do! Your Lordship's occupying
His royal place assures me of my own.

FAUST. First let the homage offered you upon
My knees find favor, Lady, in your eyes;
And let me kiss the hand by which I am
Exalted to your side. Make me co-regent
Of beauty's boundless realm and you will have
A servant, worshiper, protector, all in one!   4890

HELEN. The marvels that I see, I hear—astonishing!
The questions I should like to ask you! Why
Did that man's speech, I wonder, have so strange
A ring, strange and yet agreeable.
One sound seemed to suit itself so sweetly
To another; one word entering the ear,
Another came caressingly on its heels.

FAUST. If you like our people's way of speaking,
You'll surely be delighted with our song,
Which so delights the mind as well as ear.   4900
What we should do now is to practice it—
The to and fro of lively conversation
Gives verse encouragement and draws it out.

HELEN. Oh, it seems hard to utter speech so sweet!

FAUST. It's easy when the words come from the heart.
And when your heart's so full you cannot bear it,
You long for someone, somewhere who—

HELEN.   will share it.

FAUST. Now we look neither back nor forward, we
Find in the present—

HELEN.   our felicity.

FAUST. Our joy's our treasure, kingdom, our all,   4910
    And who will promise, swear it's so?
HELEN.   I will!
CHORUS. Who'd ever blame our Princess for the smiling face
    She shows this castle's lord? We're all captives,
    Aren't we, as we've so often been
    Since Ilium's ignominious fall and the long
    Ordeal of our wanderings on the sea.

    Women used to men's love take what comes,
    For all their connoisseurship, they can't pick
    And choose. A shepherd boy with golden curls,
    A black and bristly faun, it doesn't matter—   4920
    All are freely allowed the same rights,
    Same freedom over their lush, languid limbs.

    They lean toward one another till their knees
    And shoulders touch, clasp hands, sway blissfully
    Together on the gilded throne's upholstered seat.
    In the exuberance of happiness,
    Majesty, indifferent, proud, displays
    Its private joys before the people's eyes.
HELEN. So far away I feel, and yet so near,
    And glad, yes, more than glad that I am here.   4930
FAUST. I tremble, gasp for breath, it's all a dream,
    I'm speechless: what place am I in, what time?
HELEN. I feel both finished, done, and yet newborn,
    One piece with you, true to my dear unknown.
FAUST. Our high, rare fate, don't labor to explain it!
    Live, life demands, if only for a moment.
PHORKYAS. [*Rushing in*]
        Waste the time, do, dillydally,
        Poring over your love's story,
        Kiss and cuddle blissfully,
        Marvel at love's mystery!   4940
        Don't you feel the storm approaching,
        Hear an army's trumpets blowing,

Know that your destruction threatens?
Menelaus and his legions
March on you in hot pursuit—
Arm, arm for the bloody fight!
If they catch you, oh my goodness,
Cut you up, they will, in pieces,
Just as they did Deiphobus.
You'll pay dear for your light ladies,   4950
Those sluts soon will dance on air.
As for you, you're well aware
A sharpened ax, its edge aglitter,
Is lying ready on the altar.

FAUST. Outrageous, bursting in like this, how dis-
Agreeable! Even when grave danger threatens,
I dislike stupid, undeliberate
Haste. The most handsome messenger, if he
Comes bearing bad news, looks unlovely; and you,
Who's uglier than anybody, only love   4960
Bad news. Well, this time it won't work, you waste
Your breath: there is no danger, none. And if
There were, behold how little cause for fear we have!

[*Signal calls. Explosions from the tower. Trumpets, bugles, martial music. A mighty army marches in. The commanders, advancing from before their columns, assemble in a group.*]

Look where my captains stand together,
Heroes of many a bloody field:
He only's worthy woman's favor
Whose ready arm is her strong shield.

[*Addressing the commanders.*]

With disciplined, with fierce, mute anger,
Unconquerable battle lust,
O Northern manhood's finest flower,   4970
O nonpareil youth of the East,

Who wear the lightning of bright armor,
Who break great empires like a reed—
You pass, and thunder follows after,
The earth shakes underneath your tread.

We came ashore at Pylos, Nestor,
Its old king, had died long since;
The legions ranging over Sparta
Made mincemeat of each petty prince.

Drive Menelaus in disorder   4980
Back from these walls into the sea!
There let him roam, waylay, and plunder,
A pirate's what he's meant to be.

I'm bidden by the Spartan Queen
To name you dukes. At her feet offer
The provinces that your arms win,
As vassals keep them at her pleasure.

Germans! Corinth and her bays
Is given you, as yours defend it.
Goths! Achaia's your share, seize   4990
Its rocky ground and proudly hold it.

Messenia, Saxons, is your prize!
Our Frankish forces, yours is Elis!
Let Norman galleys sweep the seas
And make her great again, Argolis!

There make your homes, alert to meet
The challenge of an enemy;
But Sparta, Helen's ancient seat,
Shall still own the supremacy.

Enjoying under your Queen's eye   5000
This land which nothing lacks in goodness,

You'll look to her authority
For confirmation, counsel, justice.

[*Faust descends, the Princes make a circle around him the better to hear his commands.*]

CHORUS. Who means to have the Queen of Beauty for
His own—look sharp is my advice to him;
Look out a good supply of arms! Perhaps
He won her with his tongue; but he'll need more
Than words to keep her his. Insinuating
Fellows will inveigle her away,
Bold raiders, striking fast, make off with her.   5010
Preventing such things calls for careful thought.

So I have only praise for our Prince,
Think better of him than of all the others,
Seeing how he's shown himself both brave
And shrewd in going out and gathering allies
Brave as himself, great captains who stand ready
To do his every bidding instantly.
Each one, in serving his own interest,
At the same time earns his Prince's gratitude,
And both win fame and glory for themselves.   5020

For who can snatch her out of her protector's
Strong grip now? She's his, and very glad
We are she is, for his great walls, surrounding
Her inside, his armies drawn up in
Defense outside, surround, defend us, too.
FAUST. To every chieftain we have given
A rich and overflowing land;
Let each march now to his own region,
The center's ours to command.

Each shall vie with each defending   5030
This wave-washed, deep-bayed all-but-island,

Whose chain of hills runs northward, joining
The southernmost spur of the mainland.

Our wish is all the tribes may find
A happy home here, long existence,
Where Helen now is Queen—the land
That was the first to know her presence,

When from the broken shell she crept
Amid Eurotas's rushes' whispers
And by her brightness blinded quite   5040
Her mother, sister, and her brothers.

—All Hellas turns to you, you only,
It offers you its flowering breast,
The earth itself is yours entirely,
But oh, let your own home stand first!

And though its mountain range's jagged peaks
Beneath the sun's chill rays are snowy still,
A thin green's showing on the rocky flanks
Where the goat wanders cropping his scant meal.

The flowing springs pour down in rushing brooks,   5050
The gorges, slopes, and meadows have turned green;
Upon the broken uplands woolly flocks,
Spreading across the pastures, can be seen.

The scattered cattle moving cautiously,
Approach the edge of the steep cliffside's fall,
But there is shelter for the herd close by
In caves that honeycomb the granite wall,

Where Pan protects them. In the cool, wet places
Of bushy clefts, nature's nymphs live hidden,

The crowding trees reach upwards with their branches 5060
Longingly, after a higher region.

This old, old forest! Mighty oaks unbending
Stand, their gnarled limbs spreading crookedly;
The gentle maples, big with sweet sap, lifting
High their leafy heads, toss playfully.

From heavy udders, in the quiet shade,
Warm mother's milk flows down for lambs and babies,
A step away fruit ripens in the field,
From hollow treetrunks golden honey oozes.

Here ease and comfort are the legacy, 5070
The round and glowing cheek, the red, ripe mouth;
Here each possesses immortality
In his descendants' happiness and health.

And thus in pure contentment, cloudless days,
The child grows up and fathers in his turn.
Amazed, we never cease to ask: Are these
High gods descended here or are they men?

Apollo, when he kept sheep, looked completely
The handsome shepherd in both form and face:
Where Nature's still unspoiled, still rules serenely, 5080
All worlds commingle, gods and men change place.

[*Sitting down beside Helen.*]
And all this we have made our own, we two;
We'll quite forget the past, unhappy, wrong!
Think what great god it was engendered you!
The first world, there, there, is where you belong.

It's not for you, immurement in a castle!
Quite near to Sparta there's a place

Where youth keeps all its vigor, is eternal:
Arcadia, our bower of bliss!

Oh, fly with me to those blest fields, discover   5090
The happiness that's your true fate!
There these thrones turn into a leafy arbor:
Be ours Arcadian freedom and delight!

A R C A D I A

The scene changes to show enclosed arbors standing against a row
of rocky caverns. A shady grove stretching to the surrounding cliffsides.
Faust and Helen are nowhere to be seen. The Chorus lie sprawled about
asleep.

PHORKYAS. How long these girls have been asleep I've no
      Idea, nor do I know if in their dreams
      They saw what I saw, bright and clear, in front
      Of me. I'll wake them up and quite astonish
      The young things. —Astonish you, too, sitting down
      Below, you old folk waiting in suspense
      To see the outcome of these miracles.   5100
      —Wake, sleepy heads, and shake your tangled locks!
      Sit up, don't blink so, listen to my words!
CHORUS. Tell us, oh do, yes, the wonders that you say have taken place,
      Best of all we'd love to hear things unbelievable and strange,
      For how boring just to sit here staring at a lot of rocks!
PHORKYAS. Hardly rubbed your eyes, my children, and already bored
            to death?
      Listen, then: Inside the shelter that these arbors, grottoes, give,
      Our lord and our lady live a lovers' idyll.
CHORUS.   What,
            Inside there?
PHORKYAS.   Retreating from the public world, their wish
                  was I,
      Only I, should wait on them. And very honored I was,
            although   5110

As became a trusted servant I averted my attention,
Elsewhere looked, for roots, bark, mosses, in whose virtues I am
    skilled—
Leaving them all to themselves.

CHORUS. Why, you talk as if a whole world were inside there, woods
    and meadows,
Brooks and lakes: the tales you spin!

PHORKYAS.   Yes, it's so, you know so
                                   little!
In there there are depths unfathomed, long halls, courts and
    courts and long halls,
Which my sharp wits, searching, found out. Suddenly, however,
    laughter
Echoed through the caverns' reaches; looking, I saw a boy
    jumping
From his mother to his father, from one lap into the other.
So much coddling and caressing, silliness and fondest
    teasing,   5120
Shrieks of fun and shouts of pleasure, mirth that seemed to have
    no ending;
I was deafened by the din!
Naked, the bright spirit, wingless, like a faun but nothing
    brutish,
Sprang down to the ground—responding, it flung him high in
    the air,
Then a second, third leap bore him up, up till he touched the
    vaulting.
Worriedly, his mother shouted, "Leap as often as you want to,
But take care, you hear, no flying! Flying in the air's forbidden!"
And his father likewise warned him, "In the earth, the good
    earth lies the
Mighty force that throws you upward—with the tip of your toe
    only
Touch the ground, and like Antaeus, son of earth, you'll find
    you're strong."   5130

So he bounded up the rock wall, bounced from one ledge to
    another
Like a smartly driven ball—till all at once he's gone, he's vanished
In a crevice of the cavern. Oh, I thought, we've surely lost him!
Now the mother wailed, the father did his best to reassure her.
Shifting anxiously, I stood there. Then he reappeared—I
    marveled!
Had he come on hidden treasure? For he now was nobly, grandly
Dressed in robes trimmed with bright braid.
Tassels dangled from his wide sleeves, ribbons fluttered on his
    bosom,
In his hand a golden lyre, just like a petit Apollo!
Cheerfully he walked up to the overhanging ledge's brink;   5140
We're amazed, the happy parents rapturously hug each other.
Round his head what's that that's glowing? What shone so is
    hard to say.
Gold, perhaps, or the bright glow of a great mind's transcendant
    power?
In his boyish gestures, movements, it's foretold already he shall
Be the master of whatever's lovely, pleasing, beautiful,
One whose every member pulses with the eternal melodies.
Just so you'll now hear him, see him, mouths agape with
    wonderment.
CHORUS.
    Call that a wonder,
    Woman of Crete?
    Never listened when poetry   5150
    Sang its sweet lessons?
    Ionia's, Hellas's rich store of
    Legends of gods and great heroes—
    Never heard them?

    Nothing that's done today's
    Anything more than a pitiful
    Echo of long-ago glories.

Nothing, your story, compared with the
Fable, more persuasive than truth,
That's sung about Maia's son.   5160

Newborn, the baby, trig and
Tricksy already, was swaddled in
Purest down, wrapped tight in royal stuff
By the little-suspecting crowd of
Tongue-wagging nurses.
But the sly little rascal drew
Limber limbs out from their purple
Confinement and left the tight
Bindings to lie where they were—
Like the butterfly cleverly slipping its   5170
Chrysalid bondage to wave its wings
Impishly in the sunshiny air.

Nimblest of spirits, not delaying
A moment, he showed by the cunningest
Ruses he was patron of rascals
And thieves and of all those who study
What will gain them advantage—he stole
From the sea god his trident, the sword out of
Ares' sheath, bow and arrows from
Under the nose of bright Phoebus,   5180
Hephaestus his fire tongs; he even
Had made off with Zeus's dread lightning
But for fear of the fire. Eros,
However, he tripped up and beat
In a wrestling match; and the Cyprian's
Girdle, while she petted him fondly,
He quietly lifted.

[*The charming music, pure and melodious, of stringed instruments
sounds from the cavern. All listen, seeming deeply moved. From here till
the pause marked below, with full orchestral accompaniment.*]

PHORKYAS.

Listen to that lovely music,
Better than mythology!
Your gods, elderly and antique,   5190
Give them up, they're now passé.

Those old tales to us mean nothing,
We aim at a higher goal:
Only a heart full of feeling
Moves the heart and makes it feel.

[*She retreats to the cliffs.*]

CHORUS.

If a monster like yourself feels
Moved by these seductive airs,
We who've just gone through such perils
May allow ourselves some tears.

Let it go out, the sun's fire,   5200
If light dawns inside our souls,
In our own hearts we'll discover
What the outer world withholds.

[*Helen, Faust, and Euphorion dressed as above.*]

EUPHORION.

Hear a child sing, full of laughter,
And its mirth becomes yours, too;
See me leaping to the measure,
And your parent's heart leaps, too.

HELEN.

Love's delight's a human rapture
When it joins two happily;
Its delight's divine, however,   5210
When another makes it three.

FAUST.

Our cup of bliss runs over,

I am yours and you are mine;
By love we are bound together—
May it be so for all time!

CHORUS.

These two shall enjoy a million
Blessings in the gentle glow
Of the dear boy. Oh, their union,
Pledged forever, moves me so!

EUPHORION.

I'll leap and jump, I will,   5220
Up, up, I'll fly until
I touch the sky!
Immense the longing
I am seized by!

FAUST.

Careful, oh careful!
If you're too rash you'll
Crash to the ground,
And by your fall pull
All of us down.

EUPHORION.

No, I won't stay here,   5230
An earthbound creature,
Let go of me,
My hands, curls, clothing—
They're mine, I say!

HELEN.

Think, think whose child you are,
Don't make us suffer more
Than we can bear
By your destroying
The threesome we are!

CHORUS.

Shortlived, your threesome,   5240
Is what I fear!

HELEN AND FAUST.

> Bridle that violence,
> Reckless extravagance,
> For love of us;
> Bless with your presence this
> Pastoral place!

EUPHORION.

> For your dear sakes, yes,
> I acquiesce.

[*Winding in and out among the Chorus and drawing them into a dance.*]

> Round and round, see how I
> Float feather-light,   5250
> Have I the melody
> And the step right?

HELEN.

> Yes, darling, so well done!
> Lead them, each pretty one,
> Round and around.

FAUST.

> I'm not amused by this
> Spinning round, giddiness—
> How will it end?

[*Singing and dancing, Euphorion and the Chorus turn in an intricate dance.*]

CHORUS.

> When you sway your two arms
> So gracefully,
> Tossing your shining curls   5260
> So charmingly,
> When with so light a foot
> You turn and turn about,
> Forwards and backwards go,

Now spinning fast, now slow,
Then you have gained your goal,
Enchanting child:
All of us heart and soul
By you enthralled!

[*Pause.*]

EUPHORION.

Fleet-footed does, each one,   5270
You seem to me,
Ready for sport, to run
Shrieking away!
I am the huntsman,
You are the prey.

CHORUS.

No need to race like mad
In a wild chase,
Catch the doe and she's glad,
A willing prey,
For we so long to kiss   5280
You, pretty boy!

EUPHORION.

Off through the woods pellmell,
Over hill, over dale!
I find it tedious,
An all-too-effortless,
Quick victory—
Only what's seized by force
Ever suits me.

HELEN AND FAUST.

What excitement, wild commotion!
Small hope here of moderation.   5290
Are those horns that we are hearing,
Through the woods and valleys blaring?
What an uproar, what shrieks, cries!

CHORUS. [*Running in one by one*]

Like an arrow he shot past us,

Turned his nose up, he did, at us,
Chased the one who's most rampageous.
There he comes now with his prize.
EUPHORION. [*Carrying in a young girl*]
See the amazon I've got here,
I will make her serve my pleasure,
Hug her, squeeze her, though she's loath,   5300
Kiss her on her shrinking mouth—
Show the creature who is master.
GIRL.
Let me go! Inside me there's
Strength of mind, a hardy spirit
With a will as strong as yours.
Caught, am I? Well, wait a minute,
You are much too confident
Of your strength. Don't unloose me,
You will get your fingers burnt.
Ready, fool? The fun this gives me!   5310

[*Fire envelops her and she flames upwards.*]

Follow me where breezes blow,
Or where caverns yawn below,
Catch me if you can, oh let's see!
EUPHORION. [*Shaking off the last of the flames*]
I feel imprisoned here,
Pent in by bush and cliff,
It's not for me whose youth
Needs room, needs light and air.
I hear the winds' shrill cry,
Waves roaring, far away—
Would I were there!   5320

[*He springs higher and higher up the rocks.*]

HELEN, FAUST, AND CHORUS.
Daring as a mountain goat!
If you fall?—oh dreadful thought!

EUPHORION.

> I must keep on climbing higher
> So I'm able to see farther!
> Yes, I see now just where I am,
> In the middle of an island,
> Pelops's isle: on one side water,
> And the mainland on the other.

CHORUS.

> Wouldn't you rather stay
> Here where it's peaceful?   5330
> We'll go about each day
> Searching the fruitful
> Hillsides where grapevines grow,
> Apple trees, fig trees, too.
> Here where all's mildness, still
> Be mild as well!

EUPHORION.

> Dreaming of peace, are you?
> Dream if it pleases you!
> The watchword's war, the cry
> "On, on to victory!"   5340

CHORUS.

> If when there's peace,
> You wish for war instead,
> Then you confess
> All your brave hopes are dead.

EUPHORION.

> Men whom this land has taught
> By its unhappy plight
> Courage and hardihood,
> Men prompt to shed their blood—
> Draw your swords boldly,
> Into the fray!   5350
> Rescue your country
> From its decay!

CHORUS.

See how high he's climbed, no longer
Seems a little boy at all,
Cased in armor, keen to conquer,
Glittering in bronze and steel!

EUPHORION.

Trust no more to walls for shelter,
In yourselves place all your trust,
There's no citadel securer
Than a brave man's steel-ribbed breast.   5360
Do you long to live in freedom?
People arm, into the field!
Amazons be all your women,
And a hero every child!

CHORUS.

Let sacred poetry
Upwards soar, higher fly,
Shine, shine, O fairest star,
Ever more distantly,
Yet always reaching us,
Here on earth, with a voice   5370
Lovely to hear.

EUPHORION.

No, I'm no pretty child any more—
A young man armed, a soldier to fear!
Side by side with the bold I'll march boldly—
What deeds I've done in my mind already!
Now I am off,
Feet on the path
Of glory stretching onwards before me!

HELEN AND FAUST.

Barely born into the light,
Blinking still in the bright morning,   5380
You look from your dizzy height
And long for scenes of strife and suffering.

We mean nothing,
It would seem.
Was our union just a dream?

EUPHORION.

Far out at sea the cannons thunder,
The valleys echo with the din,
Afloat, afield, the hosts encounter
Each other—hear the groans of pain!
Death is duty,   5390
So it must be,
Useless for you to repine.

HELEN, FAUST, AND CHORUS.

Oh, how dreadful! Grief, oh grief!
Death you think's your duty? You!

EUPHORION.

Should I stand aside, aloof?
No, I'll share men's pain and woe.

HELEN, FAUST, AND CHORUS.

O spirit rash, alarming!
We fear a tragic ending.

EUPHORION.

I will, I will! —Now watch and see
How my wings spread gloriously!   5400
There I'll go, I must, I must!
Don't forbid what I want most!

[*He throws himself out into the air, his garments sustain him for a
moment; his head, illumined, leaves a trail of light behind.*]

CHORUS.

Icarus, Icarus!
Oh, but how sad it is!

[*He falls, a handsome youth, at his parents' feet, resembling in
death a well-known figure; his mortal part instantly fades, but the
aureole rises cometlike into the heavens. Dress, cloak, and lyre are left
lying on the ground.*]

HELEN AND FAUST.
>First we know gladness,
>Soon after, what pain!

EUPHORION'S VOICE. [*From below*]
>Mother, in darkness
>Don't leave me alone!

[*Pause.*]

CHORUS. [*Elegy*]
>No, you'll never be alone, for
>Knowing you as we think we do,   5410
>How should we forget you ever?
>Always in our hearts we'll keep you!
>Mourning, here, seems hardly called for,
>Envy's rather what we feel:
>Both as singer and as soldier
>Your star shone through well and ill.

>Blessed with all good things by birth,
>Noble forebears, health, and strength,
>Soon you lost hold of yourself,
>Killed the bloom of your bright youth.   5420
>Felt with every warm heart warmly;
>Saw the world with cool, clear eyes;
>Loved fine women passionately;
>Had a voice uniquely yours.

>Scorning law and moral custom,
>Rushing onwards recklessly,
>You found, looking round, that you'd been
>Cast out of society.
>But at last a great endeavor
>Braced your soul with earnest purpose;   5430
>Glory now was what you strove for—
>But you failed, death took you from us.

Who succeeds? Veiled destiny
Turns away and gives no answer
On this most unhappy day
When all, stricken, mutely suffer.
—Sing, however, new songs, don't
Droop your heads disconsolately;
Earth is song, and from that fount
Song pours out perpetually.   5440
                    [*Complete pause. The music stops.*]

HELEN. [*To Faust*] An old saying's truth is once again,
    Alas, confirmed in me: happiness
    And beauty are never partners very long.
    It's severed now, my bond to life, to love.
    Mourning both, saying a painful goodbye,
    I throw my arms around you one last time.
    —Persephone, receive my boy and me!

[*She embraces Faust, her corporeal shape fades, and he is left
holding her dress and veil.*]

PHORKYAS. [*To Faust*] Keep a good, firm grip on what's still left!
    That dress there, don't let go of it. They've started
    Tugging at it, demons have, already,   5450
    Would like to drag it down to Hell. Hang on!
    It may not be the goddess that you lost,
    Yet it's divine: a priceless favor you
    Should use to raise yourself aloft into
    The upper air, high, high above all that
    Is commonplace, as long as your life lasts.
    —We'll meet again, but far away from here.

[*Helen's garments, dissolving into clouds, envelop Faust, carry him
aloft, and pass away into the distance. —Phorkyas gathers up
Euphorion's dress, cloak, and lyre from the ground, comes forward to the
foot of the stage, holds them up, and speaks.*]

    A lucky find! No matter that
    The flame's no more, the fire out,

It's not the funeral of poetry. 5460
With these I'm able to consecrate
Many a tin-eared laureate,
Whole schools of them, all green with jealousy.
So if I can't supply the divine fire,
At least I can lend them the right attire.

[*She sits down beside a column at the front of the stage.*]

PANTHALIS. Girls, hurry! We are free at last of that
Thessalian witch's barbarous magic, free
Too of that tinkling music, uncouth speech,
So disconcerting to the ear and even more
The mind. —Now down to Hades! Our Queen 5470
Has gone that way already, with a solemn
Tread. As her faithful servants we
Must follow her below at once. Before
The throne of the Inscrutable Ones we'll find her, there.
CHORUS.
Wherever they are, it's fine for queens, oh yes!
Even in Hell their place is first,
Mixing proudly with their peers,
Familiars of Persephone;
We however, far back, lost
In sickly fields of asphodel, 5480
Straggling poplars, barren willows
Our sole company—how are we
Supposed to pass the time?
Squeaking miserably like bats,
Uttering ghostly whimpers, sighs?
PANTHALIS. Who's won no name, pursues no lofty ends,
Belongs to Nature's elements—depart!
It's with the Queen I long to be—not great
Works only, loyal hearts preserve us in our person.
ALL. We're given back into the light of day! 5490
No longer persons, to be sure,
We know it, feel it, yet—

Never to go back to Hades, ever!
Nature, undying, eternal
Claims us as her own spirits,
As we for our part claim her.

A PART OF THE CHORUS.

In these thousand trembling branches through which there's a
    rippling, rustling,
Wooingly we coax the springs of life from roots where they lie
    buried
To the twigs which we dress first with leaves, then blossoms,
    prodigally;
In the breezy air all's free to grow and ripen, swelling
    plumply.   5500
When the fruit falls right away the people run here and the cattle
Happily, the men to gather and the beasts to browse and nibble
And about us all are bowed down as all bowed to the first gods.

ANOTHER PART.

In these smooth, sheer cliffsides that reflect the light into the
    distance
Our dear home is where we move in soft, caressing waves of
    sound:
Ears attuned to every bird note, reedy piping of the rushes,
Even to Pan's frightful shout, our answer always ready, prompt.
When there's rustling back we rustle, thundering, our rolling
    thunder
Rumbles after, shaking, growling, twice, thrice, ten times
    through the sky.

A THIRD PART.

Sprites who are less sedentary, we run with the running
    brooks in   5510
Eagerness to reach those lush hills stretching far away below us.
Downwards tumbling then meandering, watering sloping
    meadows, later
Level pastures, lastly gardens that surround the dwelling places.
Towering high above the landscape slender tops of cypresses

Mark the course of our waters down to the broad sea's bright
    mirror.

A FOURTH PART.

Go you others where you please but here on these close-planted
    hillsides
We will whisper round the grapevines greening on their stakes
    and watch
Vintagers who daily give their heart and soul, intense devotion,
To a task whose outcome's always plagued by such uncertainty.
Using hoe and sharp spade, heaping up the earth and pruning,
    binding,   5520
All the gods they supplicate but the bright sungod most of all.
Lazy Bacchus, languid, little cares about his faithful servants,
Nods in arbors, lolls in grottoes babbling nonsense to a faun.
What he needs for his half-drunken reveries he has about him
Stored in wineskins, jars, all sorts of vessels standing right and left
In the coolness of deep caves which keep the wine through the
    long ages.
When, however, all the gods but chiefly Helios have breathed
On the vines, have wet them, warmed them, shone with
    summer's heat upon them,
Heaping cornucopias up with ruddy grapes to overflowing,
Suddenly there's coming, going: where the lone vinedresser
    labored,   5530
Vines are shaking, men are running up and down among the
    rows.
Baskets creak and buckets clatter, panniers groan and all move
    toward the
Great vat and the treaders' dance. And so the sacred vine's pure
    wealth of
Fruit is rudely trampled to a foaming, splashing, nasty pulp.
Now ear-piercing cymbals' brazen clashing's heard and Dionysus
From the mysteries appears and after him goat-footed satyrs
Whirling their goat-footed women while the long-eared beast
    Silenus

Rides, brays frantically among them. No respect for anything! All
Decency by cloven hoofs is trampled down, all senses whirling,
All ears deafened hideously! Drunken creatures grope for
    cups,   5540
Heads and bellies filled to bursting, and though here and there
    some cry out
Apprehensively it only makes the tumult louder, madder,
For to lay up new wine the old wineskins must be emptied fast.
                                [*The curtain falls.*]

[*Phorkyas, seated stage front, stands up giantlike in her buskins,
steps out of them, and takes off her mask and veil, revealing herself as
Mephistopheles—who is ready if required to offer as an epilogue his
comments on the action.*]

ACT IV

HIGH MOUNTAINS

Grim, jagged peaks.
A cloud appears, draws up to the cliffside, and settles on an
overhanging ledge. The cloud parts and Faust steps out.

FAUST. Looking down into profoundest solitudes,
    I quit the cloud that bore me gently over
    Land and sea and through fair skies, and cautiously
    Step out onto this summit's brink. Unscattered,
    The fleecy mass draws back and slowly passes
    Eastwards, my eyes straining after it
    In wonder how it shifts, divides, and changes.   5550
    But isn't that a shape it's taking? —Yes,
    My eyes don't play me false. On sunlit pillows
    Gloriously stretched out, I see a woman's
    Form, gigantic, goddesslike! Like Juno's,
    Leda's, yes, like Helen's, majestic and so lovely,
    Too, it hovers in the air. Alas,
    How soon dissolving into formlessness
    And hanging in the eastern sky like far-off
    Alps of ice—a dazzling symbol showing
    Their great meaning, the days but just now fled.   5560

    Yet round my breast and brow a shining wisp
    Of cloud still hovers, cheering, cool, caressing.
    Wavering upwards high and higher, denser
    Gathered, it seems something—what? Do I
    Deceive myself or do I see an image,
    Rapturous, of what, when I was young,
    I most loved, now lost and gone
    From me these many years? The first, the fondest
    Feelings of my heart pour up from the depths:

Its morning love, these early feelings were,   5570
The larklike, soaring joy, that instantly felt,
Scarcely understood first look which if
One could keep hold of it would shine more bright
Than all else dear! The lovely figure, showing
Forth more perfect and more perfect still
As beauty of the soul, entire, undissolved,
Ascends into the higher regions drawing
With it what is best within myself.

[*A seven-league boot comes thumping down, another following it
immediately. Mephistopheles climbs out of them and steps down. The
boots go striding off.*]

MEPHISTO. I call that making tracks, I do!
But tell me what possessed you to   5580
Light down in this horrid place
Of towering rock and black abyss?
How well I know it—from elsewhere;
Actually, it's Hell's old floor.
FAUST. You're always ready with some stupid story!
It's got no end, your Devil's repertory.
MEPHISTO. When the Lord God—most understandably—
From Heaven hurled us down into Hell's pit,
Whose central fire flamed eternally
And gave off more than enough light and heat,   5590
We devils found ourselves uncomfortably
Packed close together. All began to sweat
And huffed, from top, from bottom, to blow the fire out.
Hell filled to bursting suffocatingly
With a sulfurous stink. The acrid gas,
Expanding with immense Tartarean force,
Exploded, shattering with a thunderous blast,
Thick as it was, earth's flat, granitic crust.
This made a change, it did, in terra firma:
What once was infra, raised up, now is supra.   5600
It also showed how right it is, our theory,
Which holds things need to be turned topsy-turvy;

Which theory following, we've fled our prison
Underground to exercise dominion
In the air. An open secret, well concealed,
Which only recently has been revealed.   [*Eph. 6:12*]
FAUST. I don't ask mountains what and where they came from;
Enough they're there, so noble, brooding, awesome.
When Nature made herself out of herself,
With her own hand she shaped the rotund earth,   5610
In soaring peaks and steep rock falls rejoiced;
The mountains linking in great ranges first,
She then formed hills that they might slope down gently
By slow declension to the fertile valley,
Where all is a green garden. Kindly Nature
Has no use for eruptions, violence, fire.
MEPHISTO. You don't say! For you it's all so plain—
But we know better who were on the scene.
The abyss boiled over, flames shot to the sky,
And Moloch's hammer, lifted up on high,   5620
Pounded crags and cliffs into rock piles
And scattered lumps of mountain round for miles.
Strange boulders strew the landscape from all over.
What hurled them there? Try and explain such power!
Philosophers cannot account for it,
The huge rocks sit there and that's that,
We rack our brains and all to no result!
But common people, sturdy and upright,
Hold fast to their traditional understanding;
Their wisdom's old, goes back to the beginning.   5630
They have no doubt it is a miracle
For which great Satan is responsible.
Upon their crutch of faith, in pious pilgrimage,
They hobble to the Devil's Rock, the Devil's Bridge.
FAUST. I needn't now rely upon conjecture:
I know the Devil's point of view on Nature.
MEPHISTO. Nature! Nature! She's as it may be.
It's a point of honor, this, with me—
I was there! We people are the ones

For bringing off the most tremendous schemes!   5640
Unreason, turmoil, violence—behold the signs!
But never mind, I have a question for you:
Does everything on our earth simply bore you?
You've looked far out from this height, seen unfurled
The glory of the Kingdoms of this World.   [*Matt. 4:8*]
Though you're so hard to please, so fussy,
There must be *something* suits your fancy.
FAUST. Yes, a great thing, grandiose!
    Guess if you can what it is.
MEPHISTO. Easily done, I am sure.   5650
    Myself, I'd find some city where
The center swarms with people scrambling
Every way to make a living;
Crooked alleys, pointed gables;
In the close-built market square
Stands heaped high with vegetables;
Bloody butchers' counters where
The blowflies hover, feasting on
Fat sides of beef and venison.
We'd find there, no matter when,   5660
Such a jostling, stinking din!
To avenue next and wide square
To stroll about with lordly air;
And lastly through the city gate
To where the spreading suburbs wait,
With chaises dashing recklessly
And great crowds strolling ceaselessly—
A busy antheap overflowing
With people's restless to- and fro-ing.
Driving, riding, one would be   5670
The magnet drawing every eye,
By thousands with doffed hats saluted.
FAUST. No, that's not what I want, I!
    I'd like to see the people prosper,
In their own fashion have some pleasure,

Learn how to read, be educated
(Whose end, I fear, 's French Revolutions).
MEPHISTO. And then to build, to suit one's greatness,
An ostentatious pleasure palace,
Surrounding it with splendid gardens   5680
Whose copses, meadows, hills, hedgerows
I would in formal style dispose;
Smooth lawns, cool, shaded arbors I'd
Take care to have, allées provide;
Cascades from fall to fall descending;
A noble fountain, its jet shooting
High in the air, while round it squirting,
Petty ones are hissing, pissing;
And tucked away for pretty mistresses,
I'd put up the most charming cottages,   5690
There to while away the hours
Happily, safe from intruders.
"Mistresses," I said: you must remember
For me the feminine's a plural gender.
FAUST. Vicious, lewd—a modern Sardanapal!
MEPHISTO. Impossible, I find, to learn your will.
Your ambition aims, so it would seem,
At something highflown, bold, sublime.
You who lately voyaged through the sky,
Perhaps, moonstruck, now turn your eyes that way?   5700
FAUST. Not up but down! Here on the earth
Is opportunity enough.
My strength, my energy's unbounded,
I'll make the world sit up, astounded!
MEPHISTO. So fame is what you're after? One can see
That you've been in a heroine's company.
FAUST. Wealth, property I'll win, and power!
The doing's all and fame is nothing.
MEPHISTO. Yet there'll be poets more than willing
To sing your posthumous fame, inspiring   5710
By folly more folly, ever and ever.

FAUST. Condemned to sneer and jeer and taunt,
How should you know what men want?
Your hateful nature, hostile, bitter,
How should it know what men require?
MEPHISTO. Oh well, Doctor, do just as you please.
Let's hear how far they go, your mad ideas.
FAUST. My glance wandering to the open sea,
I saw the proud waves towering in the air,
Then roaring fall upon the level shore   5720
In furious assault, presumptuously.
And I was vexed—a mind that's free and prizes
Justice, right, finds arrogance arouses
Passionate indignation in the soul.
Was it an accident? I looked more closely:
The tide, at flood, now ebbed, having gained its goal,
But on the hour back it will come surely.
MEPHISTO. [*To the audience*]
For me the tides are nothing new,
For eons I have seen them ebb and flow.
FAUST. [*Continuing passionately*]
The water creeps up, flooding stealthily,   5730
Sterile itself, it spreads sterility.
It flows along, rising to inundate
The lowland bogs, brackish and desolate.
The waves come rolling in again and again
And then recede—with what result, what gain?
Running uncontrolled, the element
Wastes itself in vain flux and ferment.
Oh, it's enough to drive one to despair!
But I'm resolved, in spite of all, to dare
To meet the challenge of the ocean's power   5740
And force it to acknowledge me its master!

It can be done, I know. The water flows
Around, not over, any sort of rise;
A height defeats it, shallows draw it down.

The which observing, I've devised a plan
Whose execution, let success but crown it,
The satisfaction I should have! I'll bar
The lordly sea out from the lowly shore,
Restrict its power, for so long unlimited,
And drive it back upon itself, defeated!   5750
I've thought it out, the whole thing, step by step.
That's what I wish. I challenge you to help!

[*Drums and martial music in the distance, from behind the
audience's right.*]

MEPHISTO. It's easy. —Listen, those are drums I hear.
FAUST. War again! Who's wise and welcomes war?
MEPHISTO. War or peace, the wise thing is to try
    And get what you can out of it, say I.
    You keep a sharp eye out for any profit
    Chance affords. *Your* chance is now—Faust, grab it!
FAUST. Spare me riddles, please. Just say straight out
    Exactly what it is you mean by that.   5760
MEPHISTO. While coming here, with my sharp eye I noticed
    That our good Emperor looks careworn, harassed.
    You know the man—when we put on our shows
    All that fake money led him to suppose
    The world was his to do with as he would.
    A beardless youth when he came to the throne,
    He drew the false conclusion that he could
    Amuse himself and at the same time reign,
    Agreeably uniting "would" and "should."
FAUST. What a wrong idea! A ruler must   5770
    In rulership find all his satisfaction,
    Nurse a lofty purpose in his breast,
    But keep it hidden from all those about him.
    What privately in trusted ears is whispered,
    Is done—and the whole world's dumbfounded.
    And so his august will remains supreme:
    To frolic with familiars lowers him.

MEPHISTO. That's not our one! For he had fun, he did,
    While into anarchy the whole realm slid:
    Great and small in every region warring,   5780
    Brother brother banishing and killing,
    Castle against castle, town against town,
    The guilds, nobility at daggers drawn,
    And the bishop feuding with his diocese.
    Let eye meet eye, at once you're enemies;
    Throats cut in church; merchants and travelers
    The prey of roving bands of highway robbers.
    Bolder and bolder all grew, living meant:
    "On guard! Defend yourself!" —And so it went.
FAUST. Yes, went—it staggered, fell, lurched to its feet,   5790
    Stumbled a step, collapsed into a heap.
MEPHISTO. You dared not say how dreadful these things were.
    Each could and would claim full rights for himself;
    The humblest acknowledged no superior;
    Till it proved too much for the men of worth,
    Who rose up in a body and declared:
    "We've got to have for our sovereign lord
    Someone strong enough to establish order.
    The Emperor never will, he can't,
    So let us put it to a vote   5800
    And choose the realm an abler ruler,
    A man to infuse it with fresh spirit,
    Assure each subject's safety in it,
    Create a new world, one in which
    Peace and righteousness embrace.
FAUST. I hear the priestly note.
MEPHISTO.   And right you are!
    The priesthood's bellies were their biggest care;
    More than all others they provoked the tumult,
    Archiepiscopally blessing revolt and riot.
    And now the monarch whose life we made merry   5810
    Prepares to fight his last fight, as it may be.

FAUST. I pity him, the man was open, kind.

MEPHISTO. Well, while there's life there's hope, so we must find
  A way out for him from this narrow valley.
  Save him now, he'll never need to worry.
  The dice fall who knows how; if fortune favors,
  In droves he'll see come back all his supporters.

[*They cross a lower spur of the mountains to observe the disposition
of the army in the valley. Drums and martial music sound below.*]

MEPHISTO. He's taken up, I see, a good position;
  With our help, victory is certain.

FAUST. What's the point of it, tell me?   5820
  Tricks! Illusion! Sorcery!

MEPHISTO. The point? The point, dear sir, 's to win.
  Keep in mind your great aim
  And lay your plans accordingly.
  Put him back upon his throne
  And be rewarded generously.
  You'll kneel before him: grateful for his kingdom,
  He'll grant you endless seashore as your fiefdom.

FAUST. So much you've done already, so
  Go on and win a battle, too.   5830

MEPHISTO. No, that's your job, not mine at all!
  You're the Commanding General.

FAUST. Really, that's the limit, I must say;
  Commanding men is not my métier.

MEPHISTO. Your General Staff will see to that;
  General Faust won't be caught out.
  I've acted in anticipation,
  Well aware of war's confusion,
  And got together a war staff
  Composed of ancient, primitive   5840
  Mountain men. With them upon your side
  You'll never need to feel afraid.

FAUST. Who are those armed men I see?

Roused up, have you, all the mountain people?
MEPHISTO. No. Like Peter Quince in the English play,
    Only those who are most essential.

[*Enter the Three Mighty Men (2 Sam. 23:8).*]

    And here they are, my bully boys,
    One young, one middle-aged, one ancient;
    Armed differently, in different clothes,
    You won't find them a disappointment.   5850

                           [*To the audience.*]
    Today we're so delighted, all,
    By medieval knights in armor;
    These brutes are allegorical,
    Which is quite right, for so they're apter.
RAUFEBOLD. [*("Fight-hard") Young, lightly armed, gaily dressed*]
    If someone only looks at me,
    I black his eye and punch his nose for him,
    And when the coward turns to flee,
    I grab his long hair streaming after him!
HABEBALD. [*("Grab-quick") In his prime, well armed, richly dressed*]
    A stupid business, all such brawling,
    A waste of time, of precious effort.   5860
    Take all you can and keep on taking,
    All else can wait till there's time for it!
HALTEFEST. [*("Hold-fast") Old, heavily armed, without a doublet*]
    You don't end up that way the winner either!
    You live, you spend, and all's soon gone.
    It's fine to take, but keeping is much better!
    So put your trust in this old one.
    [*They go down the mountainside together.*]

IN THE FOOTHILLS

Drums and martial music below. The Emperor's tent is being pitched.

Emperor. Commander-in-Chief. Imperial Guard.

COMMANDER-IN-CHIEF. Our battle plan still seems a good one to me:
    To pull back, concentrating our whole force
    Inside the narrow confines of this valley.
    I'm full of hope. It's right, I feel, our choice.   5870
EMPEROR. Soon enough we'll see if you are right.
    But I dislike what looks like a retreat.
COMMANDER-IN-CHIEF. Only observe our right flank, Sire:
    Terrain exactly as you would desire,
    Not steep, but not ground easy to traverse,
    Better for us, and for the enemy worse.
    Its hummocks half concealing our force,
    They'll think twice before they risk their horse.
EMPEROR. What can I say? I give it my approval.
    On this field our arms must prove their mettle.   5880
COMMANDER-IN-CHIEF. Here in the center where the ground is flat
    You see the phalanx, cheerful, full of fight,
    Their tall pikes flashing in the morning haze
    Through which the bright sun darts his golden rays.
    How the close-martialed, dark square sways and heaves,
    Its thousands all on fire to do great deeds!
    Judge for yourself our strength, with your own eyes;
    I don't doubt it will split the enemy's.
EMPEROR. It's the first time I have seen it, really;
    A force like that could cope with twice as many.   5890
COMMANDER-IN-CHIEF. Our left's secure, a picked detachment holding
    The rugged heights—Sir, see their weapons gleaming!
    They guard the narrow pass into the valley;
    The enemy, caught there, as I think likely,
    Unawares, dismayed and forced to fight,
    Will see his army go down to defeat.

EMPEROR. See where they come, false kinsmen all, who called
    Me uncle, nephew, brother, who allowed
    Themselves an ever bolder liberty,
    Stole from the throne its strength and sanctity,   5900
    Fell out among themselves, laid waste the Empire,
    And now rebelling, march on me together!
    The people waver, don't know what to do,
    And where the current carries them, they go.
COMMANDER-IN-CHIEF. I sent two men I trust, out reconnoitering,
    And here one comes. May his news prove encouraging!
FIRST SPY.
        Brave and cunning as we are,
        We succeeded in our mission,
        But our news is bad, I fear:
        Many princes swear devotion   5910
        To Your Highness but extenuate
        Their inaction by the reason
        Of the turmoils in their state.
EMPEROR. To play it safe, they reckon, is being shrewd;
    Who cares for honor, duty, gratitude?
    They see their neighbor's house catch fire, burn,
    And never think it might come to their turn.
COMMANDER-IN-CHIEF. And here's the second one, slowly
        descending,
    Panting with weariness, all his limbs trembling.
SECOND SPY.
        First we saw, with much delight,   5920
        Wild confusion everywhere,
        Then were startled by the sight
        Of a new-crowned Emperor.
        Forming up in close order,
        All the crowd marched out in step
        Following their lying banner
        Like a flock of docile sheep.
EMPEROR. I'm pleased with this false emperor, believe me;
    At last I feel myself the Emperor really!

I donned my armor as a thing required,   5930
But now I wear it as a man inspired.
Our brilliant festivals, where nothing wanted,
Yet wanted danger—the only thing *I* wanted.
You had me tilting tamely at a ring—
With pounding heart, I imagined the real thing.
You vetoed wars, or otherwise my name
Would now shine starlike with a hero's fame.
When round about me the hot fire burned,
Mirroring me to myself, I felt confirmed
In my full manhood; the flames furiously   5940
Leaped at me, and though sham flames they seemed
Fierce enough in truth and real to me.
The dreams I dreamt of glorious victories!
Today I'll redeem my shameful delinquencies!

[*Heralds are sent off to challenge the rebel Emperor. Enter Faust in armor, with visor half-raised, and the Three Mighty Men, armed and dressed as above.*]

FAUST. We trust our coming here, Sir, 's not unwelcome.
Though all look well, "Take care!" is a safe dictum.
It's well known to you that the mountain folk
Are skilled in rocks, read deep in Nature's book.
Abandoning the flatland ages past,
And finding mountains much more to their taste,   5950
They toil in labyrinthine caverns, dense
With gases that are metal's noble source;
They separate, combine, test, trying to
Discover things undreamt of hitherto.
By spirit power, subtly, they construct
Forms clear and crystalline, without defect;
Then in the crystal's eternal silence peering,
Perceive what in the upper world is occurring.
EMPEROR. So I have heard, and do believe, good Sir,
But fail to see how it concerns us here.   5960
FAUST. The Sabine sorcerer from Norcia, remember,

Is your devoted servant, staunch supporter.
How grim the doom that threatened him that time:
The kindling crackled, at once leapt the flame
Up the dry logs close around him stacked,
Smeared with pitch, with sticks of sulfur packed,
Nor man nor god nor even devil able
To save the poor magician in his dire peril—
Till snatched by Majesty from a fiery burial!
In Rome that was. He feels eternally   5970
Indebted to you, watches anxiously
Your fortunes' course, their windings and their turns,
Forgetting since that hour his own concerns.
For you he studies what the bright stars mean,
The secrets that the depths of earth contain.
He bade us hurry, not delaying, hither
To stand by you. Great is the mountain's power;
There Nature mightily works, supreme and free;
The priests, thick-witted, say it's sorcery.

EMPEROR. On feast days do we welcome every guest,   5980
All enter with high spirits, full of zest;
It gladdens us, the gay throngs crowding, jostling,
That fill our palace halls almost to bursting.
But doubly welcome that stout friend must be
Who rallies to our standard loyally
In the anxious hour when the foe's defiance
Is trumpeted, and our fate hangs in the balance.
Yet keep your good sword in its sheath, respecting
This moment when, the trial of arms impending,
Men by the thousands for me, against me, are marching.   5990
Oneself's the one! The throne to him belong
Who's worthy of it, in himself is strong!
And may this specter who now haunts our Empire,
Claiming the rule as his own, a vile pretender
To land, to crown, our barons' duty, all,
Be by this fist of mine sent straight to Hell!

FAUST. However that may be, Sir, it's not wise
    To risk your own life even in such a cause.
    Your helmet, golden crest, and plume protect
    The head that inflames us to smite the landsknecht.   6000
    Without the head, what good are limbs, tell me?
    Let the head nod, the limbs sink drowsily;
    If it is struck, all are struck together;
    When it recovers, all at once recover.
    The arm is quick to see and claim its right,
    Raising the shield, to save the head from hurt;
    The sword, its duty knowing, nothing slack,
    The foe's stroke parries and returns the stroke;
    The foot, partaking in its partners' luck,
    Treads briskly on the adversary's neck.   6010
EMPEROR. Just so with him my wrath would like to deal!
    I'll make his proud head serve as my footstool!
HERALDS. [*Returning*]
      Insolently, rudely, curtly
      They received us, coarsely mocking
      Our challenge, noble, courtly;
      Scornfully asked, were we joking:
      "Your man's had his day, his story
      'S now a fading echo, dying
      Weakly out here in this valley.
      'Once there was . . .' they'll soon be saying."   6020
FAUST. It's as we should have wished, who faithfully
    Will stand with you against the enemy!
    And there they come, your people, ready, eager.
    Sound the attack! The moment's in our favor.
EMPEROR. Here I supreme command resign:
                [*To the Commander-in-Chief*]
    It's in your hands now, Prince, not mine!
COMMANDER-IN-CHIEF. Then right wing forward, meet their left
      wing climbing
    Up the slope! Our fellows, young, stout-hearted,

Driving hard, will send the rash foe reeling
Helter-skelter back, completely routed.   6030
FAUST. [*Pointing to the man on his right*]
Allow this dashing hero here
To join your ranks. And never fear—
Among your troops, you'll see, he'll prove a bold knave
And show both friend and foe the stuff he's made of.
RAUFEBOLD. [*Presenting himself*]
Whoever meets me head on won't retire
Without his jaw smashed, upper also under;
Whoever turns his back on me, poor noddy,
Will find his head's been parted from his body.
And if your men pitch in while I
All about me ruin spread,   6040
I guarantee the enemy
Will drown, each one, in his own blood.

Exit.

COMMANDER-IN-CHIEF. Now let the center move and join the action,
Deploying its full strength, but with due caution.
On the right already by the fierce onset
Our men made, their battle plan's been upset.
FAUST. [*Pointing to the one in the middle*]
And here's this one. I'm glad to recommend him.
He's quick, he is, and drives the foe before him.
HABEBALD. [*Presenting himself*]
The fighting spirit of the Imperial soldier
Now be united with the thirst for plunder,   6050
All spirits fired with the same ambition:
To seize the rival Emperor's rich pavilion.
He won't, we swear, sit long on his high horse!
I'll lead the phalanx—out in front's my place.
EILEBEUTE. [*("Snatch-the-Loot") Canteen woman, snuggling up to him*]
Although we've not been hitched, we two,
He's still for me my dearest beau.
Oh what a harvest waits here for us!

A woman when she robs is ruthless,
She knows no mercy once she's started.
Then victory hurrah! And all's permitted. 6060

Both exit.

COMMANDER-IN-CHIEF.
It's just as we foresaw, they've thrown their right
Against our left with all the strength they've got.
Our men must beat back their headlong advance,
Which threatens our possession of the pass.
FAUST. [*Pointing to the one on the left*]
Then, Sir, remark this fellow. It can't hurt
To make a strong force even stronger yet.
HALTEFEST. [*Presenting himself*]
About your left you needn't fear;
Let me be there, all's warranted secure.
The grip this old man's fingers take
Not even lightning bolts can break. 6070
MEPHISTO. [*Descending from above*]
Now look behind you where from every
Cave and cavern pours an army
Crowding all the paths with hordes
In helm and harness, fiercely waving
Spears and shields and ancient swords:
A powerful reserve awaiting
Our signal to attack.

[*Aside, to the knowing ones in the audience.*]

Where are they from? Shh, not to ask!
All right, I'll tell you. I've cleared out
The dusty armories here about 6080
Where rusting they stood or they sat
Their horses, still believing that
They were the earth's almighty rulers,
Lordly knights and kings and kaisers—
Who now are only empty shells
(As empty as those once housed snails)

Which phantoms dress up in to resurrect
Old chivalry and bring the Middle Ages back.
If devils, too, have got into the act,
No matter, what counts here is the effect.   6090

[*Aloud.*]

Hear them furiously working
Themselves up into a temper, bumping
Into one another with a
Tinny sound of rattling armor.
Their tattered ensigns restlessly await
The freshening breeze to make them stand out straight.
Remember, these are an old race of people
Who long once more to breathe the dust of battle.

[*A shattering trumpet blast from above. Noticeable wavering in the
enemy's ranks.*]

FAUST. The heavens lower, in the murk
          Here and there there's a red spark   6100
          Ominously flashing out;
          Already arms gleam bloodily,
          The rocks, the forest, and the sky,
          The air around, are gules throughout.
MEPHISTO. Our right wing's showing lots of firmness;
          The giant Raufbold in their midst,
          Towering high above the rest,
          Goes workmanlike about his business.
EMPEROR. Where I saw one arm raised before,
          Now look, he's got a dozen more.   6110
          There's more than Nature at work here!
FAUST. You've never heard of the mirages
          Seen on Sicilian shores and marshes?
          Visible in the bright day,
          They hover halfway up the sky,
          Reflections in the atmosphere.
          Very strange these visions are—
          Cities floating in the air,

Gardens, too—it's all true, Sir!
Image image following,   6120
Appearing and then vanishing.
EMPEROR. But I'm uneasy, I can see
   The tips of spears eerily
   Ablaze, and little flames that dance
   Along the phalanx's every lance.
   It's too uncanny, much, for me.
FAUST. Excuse me, Sir, those are what's left of
   Spirits now defunct, inactive:
   The antique twins, the Dioscuri,
   Whom all that sail the salt sea swear by—   6130
   The fire's their last spark of life.
EMPEROR. I'd like to know whom we owe Nature's
   Kindly doing us such favors,
   Performing prodigies in our behalf?
MEPHISTO. Why, whom else but the necromancer,
   As anxious for you as a mother?
   Distressed to see you threatened by
   So powerful an enemy,
   The grateful magus harbors only one wish,
   To see you saved though he himself should perish.   6140
EMPEROR. Rome cheered me through the streets: now someone to
   Be reckoned with, I meant to show it, so,
   Without considering, on seeing that
   The ancient fellow found his seat too hot,
   Commanded his release. This spoiled a pleasure
   Dear to priests, gone was the Church's favor.
   And now long after that impulsive act,
   Do I experience its good effect?
FAUST. A rich reward attends all generous deeds.
   But upwards, Sir, direct your gaze!   6150
   I think he's sending you a sign
   Whose meaning will be made clear soon.
EMPEROR. I see an eagle soaring in the heavens,
   Hard after it one of those fearsome griffins.

FAUST. Watch, do! I'm sure the omen's favorable!
　　The griffin after all is just a fable,
　　So how should he imagine himself able
　　Ever to trade blows with a real-life eagle?
EMPEROR. Circling each other warily,
　　At the same instant suddenly　　　　　　　　6160
　　Hurtling through the air, they close
　　And make the feathers fly with their sharp claws.
FAUST. The wretched griffin, mauled, discomfited,
　　His lion's tail abased, has plummeted
　　Down into the trees upon the height
　　And disappears ingloriously from sight.
EMPEROR. As you read the sign, so be it!
　　Struck with wonder, I accept it.
MEPHISTO. [*Looking to the right*]
　　One hard assault after another
　　Has made the enemy retire,　　　　　　　　　6170
　　Putting up a scattered fight
　　As he is forced back on his right
　　So that his ranks, dismayed, confused,
　　Leave his main troops' left exposed.
　　And now our phalanx, moving rightward,
　　With lightning speed drives its spearhead
　　Right at his weak spot. And just as
　　Waves the howling storm wind raises
　　Mountain high, contend together,
　　The two sides have at one another.　　　　　　6180
　　It couldn't have been better planned,
　　The day is ours, a famous victory gained!
EMPEROR. [*Looking left, to Faust*]
　　Look that way, over there, however;
　　Our position seems in danger.
　　I can't see stones being pitched
　　At the foe, who has reached
　　The lower height; above, the cliff
　　Looks abandoned, without life.

The foe advances near and nearer,
Overwhelming in his number, 6190
The pass, I fear, may have been taken—
A fitting end to godless efforts!
What good have they been, all your black arts?

[*Pause.*]

MEPHISTO. I see my two grim ravens coming:
What kind of news might they be bringing?
It's looking bad, is my opinion.
EMPEROR. What do they want, those ugly things,
Sailing here on their black wings
From the hot fighting on the mountain?
MEPHISTO. [*To the ravens*]
Sit at my ear, close to me, 6200
Your advice is trustworthy,
Whom you protect won't soon be beaten.
FAUST. [*To the Emperor*]
You've heard of pigeons, I am sure,
Who find their way back from afar
Unerringly to their home roost.
Now these birds, too, from a far place
Fly home with sure intelligence,
Except there is this difference:
The pigeon post we have for peace,
For war we have the raven post. 6210
MEPHISTO. Very grave this news is!
Look there at the precipice:
The foe swarms up, our heroes waver;
They've seized, I see, the neighboring height,
And if they take the pass, good night!
We'd find ourselves in hot water.
EMPEROR. So you deceived me after all!
I feel myself such a fool,
All along I feared a trap.
MEPHISTO. Courage! Never give up hope. 6220
Patience, cunning, till all's won!

It's always darkest before dawn.
I'll take command, just say the word;
My messengers wait at my side.

COMMANDER-IN-CHIEF. [*Meanwhile approaching*]
Oh but it gave me pain to see
You take these rogues for an ally.
Sorcery is a weak friend
Who smiles and fails you in the end;
All's bright at first and then all's black.
It's looking bad for us and I can't change it; 6230
They began it, well then, let them end it.
I resign, here's my staff back.

EMPEROR. Keep it till our luck improves,
As I hope. That ugly rogue's
Grinning face and raven cronies
Horrify me, my blood freezes.

[*To Mephistopheles.*]

I can't allow you the baton,
It's not for you, you're the wrong man.
But yes, by all means take command
And save us—you have a free hand. 6240

[*Retires into the tent with the Commander-in-Chief.*]

MEPHISTO. He can keep his stupid mace.
It's no use to the likes of us:
It had a thing, a cross it looked like, on it.

FAUST. So what do we do now?

MEPHISTO.   Why, we have done it!
—Off you go, my dear dun cousins, quick
And serviceable, to the lake
Upon the mountain, greet with my best wishes
The Undines sporting with the fishes,
And borrow from them their flood trick!
They are women, have the knack, 6250
Which we can't understand, to sunder

Seem from *be* so that the former
You would swear was the latter.

[*Pause.*]

FAUST. The water maidens must have yielded promptly
To our ravens' flattering tongues: already
I see water has begun
To trickle down the bare rock, soon
The trickling swells into a stream:
Their once bright hopes are looking dim!
MEPHISTO. They didn't count on being soused, 6260
Their boldest climbers drenched and doused!
FAUST. Streams unite with streams, in a great surge
Pour out of gulleys doubled in their size;
One torrent, high up, in a great arc leaping,
Falls on level rock, the water gushing,
Rushing this way, that; and so by stages
Down into the valley the flood plunges.
All resistance, never mind how brave,
Surely must be drowned in the huge wave.
I'm scared myself, so frightful such deluges. 6270
MEPHISTO. I don't see it, for it's all a hoax,
A sham I'm proof against, it only works
On human eyes; but its bizarre result
I see with pleasure: hordes of men that bolt
Away in panic fearing they'll be drowned,
Ridiculously gasping, spitting, blowing,
And making swimming motions as they're running,
When all the while what's underfoot's dry ground!
Ha, ha, confusion's rampant all around!

[*The ravens return.*]

Well done, and I will tell the Master so. 6280
But if you wish to show you're masters, too,
Off at once to where the Little People
Are busy striking sparks from stone and metal
At their glowing smithy. Talk to them

Of this and that, whatever; exert your charm
So as at last to beg from them some fire,
The very best the dwarf folk manufacture.
On any summer evening you can see
Lightning glimmering in the distant sky,
Stars shooting through the heavens, high, so high.   6290
But lightning darting through dense underbrush,
Stars on the wet ground sparking with a hiss
You don't see often, they're not commonplace.
It doesn't call for great exertions, just
Ask politely first; if no, insist.

[*The ravens leave. All happens as above.*]

Blindly stumbling in thick gloom,
The foe can't see in front of him;
Lights flashing all about, here, there,
Then suddenly a blinding glare—
Good, good, but some noise, too, we need, to scare   6300
The living daylights out of him.
FAUST. The empty armor from the musty halls
Take, in the fresh air, a new lease on life
And clank and rattle on the cliff:
How strange the noise is, unreal, false.
MEPHISTO. Right, right! There was no holding them back longer,
And now they whack away with knightly ardor
As in the good old days of chivalry.
Greaves and brassarts locked in bloody strife
Renew, as Ghibelline and Guelf,   6310
Their everlasting enmity.
For them it's a time-honored custom,
You can't ever reconcile them;
Already far and wide, my, what an uproar!
The Devil likes his revels animated,
He's found that what works best is party hatred,
Which ends at last in dreadfulness and horror.

Hear it now, the panic, screams of fright,
And mixed with them a shrill, satanic shout
Which through the valley sends a violent shudder.   6320

[*A warlike din sounds from the orchestra, passing over into lively
martial airs.*]

THE RIVAL EMPEROR'S TENT

Throne. Sumptuous interior.
Habebald. Eilebeute.

EILEBEUTE. And here we are, the very first!
HABEBALD. Show me the raven flies as fast!
EILEBEUTE. The riches here! Man, what a heap!
     Where to begin? Where to stop?
HABEBALD. So crammed with good things the place is,
     I've trouble knowing what to choose.
EILEBEUTE. I'll take this carpet. How I've had
     To make, on bare boards, my hard bed!
HABEBALD. Here's a spiked club, just the kind
     I've so long wanted, couldn't find!   6330
EILEBEUTE. A stunning scarlet cloak, gold-trimmed,
     Of the kind I've always dreamed!
HABEBALD. [*Picking up the club*]
     With this the business is soon done,
     You knock him dead and then move on.
     —Your sack's already bulging but
     There's lots better stuff than that,
     So leave it lay. Instead seize hold
     Of one of these chests filled with gold,
     Nothing but gold, to pay the army.
     Grab it up, we've got to hurry.   6340
EILEBEUTE. Murder, what a weight! I can't
     Lift it, much less carry it.
HABEBALD. That back of yours is strong—quick, stoop

And I will heave the strongbox up.
EILEBEUTE. It's slipping off, it's falling down!
You've gone and broken my backbone.

[*The box falls and breaks open.*]

HABEBALD. The gold's all spilt, a yellow heap:
Down, woman, down and pick it up!
EILEBEUTE. [*Crouching*]
I'll gather up an apronful.
We'll have a nice pile, we will, still.   6350
HABEBALD. Enough. Now off you go, my girl.

[*She straightens up.*]

Damn! Your apron's got a hole!
With every step you take you scatter
Riches round in a gold shower.
IMPERIAL GUARDS. Nosing round this place, are you?
All here's the Emperor's, it's taboo.
HABEBALD. We risked our skins, by God we'll have
Our share of what is owed the brave.
We are soldiers, custom grants
To us as spoils the foeman's tents.   6360
IMPERIAL GUARDS. That's not our way, no, not at all:
To be a soldier and to steal!
Only an honest soldier may
Fitly serve His Majesty.
HABEBALD. Your honesty's a well-known thing,
Its name is requisitioning.
We all of us ply the same trade
And "Hand it over!" 's the password.

[*To Eilebeute*]

Get going, girl, with what you've got.
For us here there's no welcome mat.   6370

[*They leave.*]

FIRST GUARD. What, I wonder, held you back
From giving that smart rogue a whack?
SECOND GUARD. Suddenly I felt so weak,

The two of them seemed so ghostlike.

THIRD GUARD. Spots danced before my eyes, the light
Was strange, I couldn't see things straight.

FOURTH GUARD. I'm at a loss what to say:
So very hot it was all day,
Oppressive, sultry, thick with fear!
Men staggering here, toppling there;   6380
Groping for the foe, you struck
And down each fell beneath your stroke;
A veil, it seemed, your eyes obscured
And in your ears it buzzed, hummed, roared.
And so things went and now we're here.
What happened? We have no idea.

[*Enter the Emperor with four Princes. The Guards fall back.*]

EMPEROR. However it was, we've won, the enemy scattered
In flight across the plain, completely routed.
Look, there's the empty throne. The traitor's treasure,
Bundled in carpets, hardly leaves room to enter.   6390
With our bodyguard around us, we await
The nations' envoys in imperial state.
Glad news come pouring in on every hand:
The people's allegiance restored, peace in the land.
Perhaps we had some unorthodox help—however,
We won in the end thanks to our own endeavor.
Accidents happen, it seems, to stand you in good stead:
A stone falls out of the sky, the foe is showered with blood;
Rumbling out of caverns an eerie, huge noise
Raises our spirits, depresses the enemy's.   6400
Defeated, he's the target of fresh derision;
Triumphant, we thank God for his protection,
Which the people echo with spontaneous shouts:
"We praise, thee, O Lord," sounds from a thousand throats.
I look within, as I've done rarely, find
A heart devoutly turned, a grateful mind.
A happy-go-lucky prince squanders his days,

The mounting years teach him to mend his ways.
For house, court, realm, without delay, therefore
We join ourself with you, O worthy four!   6410
                                                      [*To the first*]

You, Prince, disposed our forces skillfully,
And at the decisive moment struck heroically.
Now we have peace, act in all things as required.
I name you our Marshall! With the office I give you its sword!
LORD HIGH MARSHALL. Till now our business has been civil war;
   But once frontiers and throne are made secure,
   Allow me, on the days of merrymaking,
   To set the Great Hall's table for the feasting.
   I'll walk before you, hold aloft the blade:
   The sign of majesty and its safeguard.   6420
EMPEROR. [*To the second*]
   And you who unite, with gentle manners, gallantry,
   Be our Chamberlain—not an easy duty.
   Take charge, our wish is, of the household staff
   Who serve us so poorly, so constant their strife.
   Your high example teach each one the way
   To wait on his masters with due courtesy.
LORD HIGH CHAMBERLAIN. How earn your favor? By doing Your
      Highness's will:
   Helping the good, treating mildly the bad as well;
   Being plain without guile, without cunning serene;
   Just as I am, Sir, by you I'd be seen!   6430
   Let me picture for you the festive scene in the Hall:
   You come to the table, I present you the golden bowl,
   You hand me your rings, bathe your hands for the feast,
   Refreshing yourself, as I by your glance am refreshed.
EMPEROR. My thoughts are too earnest to think of enjoyment.
   No matter—it helps, does a festive commencement.
                                                      [*To the third*]

You I appoint our Lord Steward—in your care
Our game preserves, poultry yard, manor farm are!
As the season is, duly, know, Sir, I expect

To dine on my favorite dishes, well cooked.   6440
LORD HIGH STEWARD. I'll make it my pleasant duty to fast
    Till you may sit down every day to a feast.
    I'll toil side by side with the cooks in the kitchen
    To bring near the far off, the season hasten.
    But exotic things, first fruits, are not to your taste,
    What's simple, what's wholesome is what you like best.
EMPEROR. [*To the fourth*]
    Since feasting must be all our business today:
    Young hero, sheath your sword, our Cupbearer be!
    As such give your closest, most earnest attention
    To stocking our cellars with the wines we delight in.   6450
    However, you yourself must observe moderation;
    When the toasts go around, Prince, beware of temptation!
LORD HIGH CUPBEARER. Only entrust the youth with duties, and then
    Under your eyes see how quickly they grow into men.
    In my mind's eye I, too, see the great scene, Sir:
    On the sideboard I set out glittering gold, silverware,
    Reserving the noblest cup, the loveliest goblet
    For His Highness's use at the boisterous banquet:
    Rich glass of Venice aglow with the promise of pleasure,
    In it the wine is robuster yet the drinker stays sober.   6460
    But the goblet's miraculous virtue is trusted too often;
    Your Majesty's temperate nature is a surer protection.
EMPEROR. All I've declared on this solemn occasion
    You may with full confidence, Princes, rely on.
    What the Emperor promises, no one shall countermand.
    Yet a written confirmation is needed, signed by my hand.
    And here is the very man to prepare us the parchment.
    Archbishop, welcome! You come at just the right moment.

[*Enter the Archbishop-Chancellor.*]

A keystone fixed in an arch braces the structure
    So the masonry holds, keeps it standing forever.   6470
    Here my four Princes are! We have proclaimed
    How household and court henceforth must be maintained.

But now with respect to the realm as a whole: I give
The responsible power into the hands of you five.
I mean to make you preeminent in property;
And so with the lands seized from the enemy
I'm pleased to enlarge the regions your lordships won.
To each we award many a noble domain,
Also vouchsafing the right of further extension
Of the properties granted, by purchase, exchange, and
    succession.   6480
As a Peer of the Realm, each possess without let
All the prerogatives appertaining to it.
As judges your verdict is final, pronounced once for all,
No question nor challenge allowed, nor right of appeal;
Yours be all levies, rents, tolls, taxes, and fees;
From saltworks, from mines, mints, all royalties.
How grateful I am these high honors are proof
By which you are raised to be nearest myself.
ARCHBISHOP. I thank Your Majesty on their, on my behalf!
    It greatly strengthens us, also yourself.   6490
EMPEROR. I intend you five a higher honor yet.
    My life's my realm's, and I rejoice in it,
    But even as I strive ambitiously,
    I think how many have preceded me.
    I, too, must part from dear friends in due course;
    And when that day comes you must make the choice
    Of my successor. —May it bring, his election,
    To these turbulent times a good, a peaceful conclusion!
ARCHBISHOP. We glow with pride, first princes of the world,
    Knees humbly bent, obedient to your word.   6500
    As long as the blood courses in our veins
    We'll be the body your least will commands.
EMPEROR. So in conclusion: let what we have ordained
    Be written down and for all time confirmed.
    As lords hold absolute what you've been granted,
    Except your lands must never be divided.
    However you add to what you presently own,

All, all must pass unabated to the eldest son.
ARCHBISHOP. I'll gladly see to it so important a statute
To the realm, to ourselves, is speedily set down on
parchment   6510
By my Chancery's clerks, with the seal affixed to it,
So Your Majesty's sacred hand duly may sign it.
EMPEROR. And now, sirs, depart so each one of you may
Ponder what we've decreed on this great day.

[*The secular Princes withdraw; the spiritual one remains.*]

ARCHBISHOP. [*Pompously, unctuously*]
The Chancellor departs, the Bishop must not stir,
A warning spirit drives him to seek your ear!
So anxious his fatherly heart is, so deeply concerned.
EMPEROR. When all is rejoicing, what should trouble your mind?
ARCHBISHOP. It bitterly grieves me, Sire, at this hour,
To see your person leagued with Satanic power.   6520
Your throne is now safe, to be sure, or so it may seem—
Alas, in contempt of the Lord and His Vicar in Rome!
If the Pope should get wind of it, his dread anger
Would utterly shatter your iniquitous empire.
He doesn't forget how Your Grace, newly crowned,
All Christendom contumaciously scorned.
Your first act of mercy chose whom to set free?
A damnable practicer of sorcery!
But beating your breast now, from your ill-gotten treasure
Devote to things holy a trifling, small measure: 6530
This region of hills in which you erected your tent
(Where evil spirits banded to lend you support,
In whose Prince of Lies you were only too glad to believe)
For the Church's holy endeavors, piously give—
With mountains and forests as far as they reach,
And broad, upland pastures, grassy and rich,
Lakes crowded with fish, brooks, kills, streamlets that flow
Tumbling and winding to the valley below,
And the valley as well with field, dale, and chase!

That will show your repentance, restore you to grace.　　6540
EMPEROR. Oh how I've offended, I'm filled with horror!
　Fix the boundaries yourself, as you think proper.
ARCHBISHOP. Firstly, proclaim it your holy, fixed purpose
　To devote this profaned place to Heaven's service.
　Already I see stout walls rising in air,
　The light of the morning sun filling the choir,
　The transept on either side building well out,
　The great nave completed, making glad the devout,
　Who stream through the doors, full of glowing faith, all.
　For the first time the bells sound across hill and dale,　　6550
　Loud pealing from spires that heavenwards strain,
　The sinner returns to the fold, born again.
　The day, may it dawn soon, that we hallow God's house,
　Your Majesty's presence shall make glorious!
EMPEROR. By this work may my pious intention be shown
　To glorify God, cleanse my soul of its stain.
　This is well! It has raised my soul mightily.
ARCHBISHOP. There remains, Sir, a final formality.
EMPEROR. Yes, the formal conveyance of the lands to the Church—
　Present me the deed and I'll sign it at once.　　6560
ARCHBISHOP. [*Takes his leave, but then turns back*]
　Also, allow, for the cathedral we'll build, full use
　Forever of the income—tithes, taxes, and rents—they produce.
　The money we'll need to keep it up worthily!
　The outlays required to run the place properly!
　Also, to push on the work in this desolate spot
　We should want a small share of the gold from your loot.
　Moreover, I mustn't conceal the fact that
　From far off we'll have to cart timber, lime, slate.
　The hauling's the people's, urged on from the pulpit,
　The Church blesses all those who devotedly serve it.　　6570
　　　　　　　　　　　　　　　　　　　　　　Departs.
EMPEROR. The sin that I laid on my soul, Lord, is heavy!
　Those wretched magicians are costing me plenty.
ARCHBISHOP. [*Again coming back, with a deep bow*]

Your Majesty, pardon! But now I remember:
You granted that scoundrel the shores of the Empire.
These, too, must fall under the ban, Sir, unless
Penitently you assign all their income to us.
EMPEROR. [*Exasperated*]
But the land isn't there yet, it's still under water!
ARCHBISHOP. If the right's on one's side one can wait with
composure.
EMPEROR. I might as well sign the whole Empire over!

ACT V

COUNTRYSIDE WITH SEASHORE

TRAVELER.

> There they stand, each dark, old linden,   6580
> Hardy still, still flourishing—
> To see them once again, imagine,
> After years of voyaging!
> It's the same old place, same cottage
> Sheltered me when, overwhelmed
> By the stormy billows' upsurge,
> I was shipwrecked on this strand.
> I would like to thank the worthy
> Couple who took care of me;
> But so old then, is it likely   6590
> They're alive to welcome me?
> They were such kind, pious people!
> Knock, should I, or call aloud?
> —Are you there still, hospitable,
> Happy always to do good?

BAUCIS. [*A little old woman*]

> Hush, hush, Sir, my man is resting!
> Quietly, for his dear sake!
> Long sleep lends him strength for working
> In the hours he's awake.

TRAVELER.

> Mother, is it you, the one I   6600
> Owe such thanks, your man, too, both?
> By the mercy that you showed me
> In my youth, you saved my life.
> Are you Baucis, who refreshed my
> Brine-parched lips, gave me back breath?

[*Enter Philemon.*]

210

Philemon, you! Who so bravely
Dragged my goods out of the surf,
Who so quickly lit the beacon,
Rang the silver-sounding bell!
Providentially it was given   6610
You to save me from the gale.

I must walk out to the seashore,
View again the watery waste,
Fall upon my knees in prayer
To relieve my too charged breast.

[*He walks down to the dunes.*]

PHILEMON. [*To Baucis*]
Hurry now and set the table
Mid the garden's greenery.
What a shock he'll get, he'll marvel,
Swear it's all some sorcery.

[*Joining the Traveler.*]

Where the waves broke fiercely on you,   6620
Where you weltered in cruel seas,
See, a garden now receives you
As if into Paradise.
Older grown, I lacked the vigor
To pitch in, assist the work;
My strength ebbed as in like measure,
Grudgingly, the sea fell back.
Led by skillful masters, hardy
Workmen came, they diked and dammed,
Drove back waters once unruly: 6630
Rulers where the sea had reigned.
Verdant meadow upon meadow,
Wood and garden, field and town—
Look, look, let the sight delight you,
For the sun will soon go down.

Far away white sails are making
For their haven for the night,
Birdlike knowing a nest's waiting,
Confident of a safe port.
Only at the far horizon   6640
Can you glimpse the azure sea;
Roundabout are peasants, townsmen,
Agriculture, industry.

[*The three at table in the garden.*]

BAUCIS.

Speechless, are you? Though you're starving,
Letting the good soup grow cool?

PHILEMON.

What he saw wants some explaining,
You're a talker, tell him all.

BAUCIS.

Well, it was a wonder, no doubt,
But I'm troubled by it still.
For the whole thing didn't seem right,   6650
Had about it something ill.

PHILEMON.

He did wrong, the Emperor, giving
That man rule of the seashore?
Well, a herald, trumpet sounding,
Cried the news outside our door.
Close by the first steps were taken,
Tents and shacks raised near our dunes;
Soon a gleaming palace stood on
Sand now turned into green lawns.

BAUCIS.

In the daytime workmen sweated   6660
Fruitlessly with pick and spade;
In the night where blue lights flitted,
Next day there a dam was, made.
Men were sacrificed, I'm certain,
Through the dark you heard them wail;

Seawards fiery torrents spilt down,
Dawn came, there was a canal!
Godless, he's a man who itches
To possess our cottage, trees;
Overbearing in his riches,   6670
He imagines we're his slaves.

PHILEMON.
Yet he offered us good farmland
On the soil that he reclaimed.

BAUCIS.
Put no trust in what was swampland,
Stick where you are, on high ground!

PHILEMON.
Come, we'll walk out to the chapel,
Watch the sun sink to its rest,
Ring the bell and kneeling, pray, all,
Our old God in whom we trust.

FAUST'S PALACE

A large, formal garden. Broad, straight canal. Faust, now very old, walking about and thinking.

LYNCEUS THE WATCHMAN. [*Through a megaphone*]
The sun declines, the last ships cheerly   6680
Homeward steer upon the tide.
And see, in the canal a portly
Galleon has just arrived.
Her colored pennants flutter gaily,
Upon her yards swell her white sails;
The sailors speak your name devoutly,
Now brightest fortune on you smiles.

[*The bell sounds across the dunes.*]

FAUST. [*Starting*] That damned bell, malicious, gloating,
Hurts me like a blow! Before,
My vast possessions stretch unending,   6690

Behind, a molehill leaves me sore,
Reminding me what I possess is
Less than all. I feel such pique
That still escaping all my clutches
Are lindens, hut, and moldering kirk.
And if the shade there should invite me,
The thought I'd be a trespasser
Poisons all desire for me—
How I wish I were elsewhere!

WATCHMAN. The beflagged ship, borne gently by   6700
The evening breeze, draws near the quay!
Piled high upon its crowded decks
Are chests and boxes, bales and sacks.

[*A splendid ship, loaded with goods from the four corners of the earth. Mephistopheles. The Three Mighty Men.*]

CHORUS.
Home, home at last,
The harbor won!
Hurrah the Master,
Better none!

[*They disembark; the cargo is unloaded.*]

MEPHISTO. Very well our venture went,
Let him approve and we're content.
With only two ships we sailed forth,   6710
Now twenty scrape against the wharf.
The story of our deeds is told
By what comes pouring from the hold.
Far out at sea your soul is free,
Who stops to think there, uselessly?
A ship is caught as you catch fish,
What's called for's action, spirit, dash,
And when you've bagged a catch of three,
You grapple a fourth presently;
As for the fifth one—well, good night!   6720

When yours the power, yours the right.
No questions asked, what counts is what
You're able to draw in your net.
If I know maritime affairs,
What they consist of, first, are wars,
Then trade, and lastly piracy:
Inseparable trinity.

THE THREE MIGHTY MEN.

No grateful word,
No smiling welcome!
You'd think the treasure 6730
We have brought him
Smelt bad, such a
Face he pulled.
A king's ransom
Leaves him cold.

MEPHISTO.

Don't expect
More out of him.
And anyhow
You helped yourselves already.

THE THREE.

Only to 6740
Relieve our ennui.
We want, we do,
The loot shared fairly.

MEPHISTO.

First carry it
Up to the hall,
Display the lot,
The whole rich haul.
When he lays eyes on
All that plunder,
I'm sure he'll reckon 6750
Up things better
And show himself

No skinflint, he
Will entertain us
Royally.
Tomorrow brings our dear jills here,
I'll see to it they're well cared for.

[*The cargo is carried off.*]

MEPHISTO. [*To Faust*] With beetling brows, a black expression,
Is how you welcome your good fortune,
Although your wisdom's been confirmed   6760
And peace made between sea and land.
The flood, restrained, lets willingly
Your ships pass swiftly out to sea;
You can boast that from this beach
The whole world lies within your reach.
Right here the project had its start,
Right here the first rough shack was built;
Where oars now make a busy splash,
The first picks scratched a shallow ditch.
Your great purpose, your men's toil,   6770
Have won the prize of earth, sea, all.
From here—
FAUST.   Enough! How you go on!
Your *here* is why I'm so cast down.
Resourceful man that you are, listen:
It stabs me, it does, to the heart,
Unbearable, a mad obsession
I blush with shame to speak about:
They've got to go, that poor old couple—
I'll have those lindens, won't be foiled!
They're few, yet not mine, how they rankle,   6780
Spoil my possession of the world.
I meant to fix a scaffold to
The branches so that I might view
All I've accomplished, comprehend
This great achievement of man's mind

In a glance: the broad lands won
For men to build their dwellings on,
Where teeming nations now may have
The space they need to work and thrive.

This, this, is the worst torment,   6790
To have so much, yet still to want!
That bell's sound, the lindens' smell
Oppress, churchlike, tomblike, my soul.
My will, that's free and brooks no let,
A patch of sand can bring up short.
Where's the cure for this deep ache?
The bell tolls and I go beserk.
MEPHISTO. Of course, of course! Such vexation
Exasperates one out of reason,
Dear me, yes! That dinging, donging   6800
Grates on every man of feeling,
Spoils the quiet of the evening
With its bimming and its bamming,
Mixes into everything
From christening to burying,
As if between the *bam* and *bim*
Life were a mere interim.
FAUST. Their obstinacy, stubbornness,
Spoils for me my great success,
And heartsore I find that I tire   6810
Of wishing to be a just squire.
MEPHISTO. Your tender conscience! I am startled—
The populations you've resettled!
FAUST. Then clear them out, this very hour!
—You know the pretty house and garden
I picked out for them to live in.
MEPHISTO. I'll move them there and in a twinkling
They'll be happily housekeeping.
Set them up in a nice cottage,
They'll forgive us the rough usage.   6820

[*He whistles shrilly. The Three appear.*]

You hear his Lordship! Go on, do it!
Tomorrow we will have our banquet.

THE THREE. The old boy greeted us so dourly;
A lively feast is our due, surely.

MEPHISTO. [*To the audience*]
How humankind keeps on and on!
It's Naboth's vineyard once again.   [*1 Kings 21*]

DARK OF NIGHT

LYNCEUS THE WATCHMAN. [*Singing from the lookout*]
Born sharp-eyed and called
To watch from this tower,
I look at the world
With such delight, pleasure!   6830
Afar off I peer,
Look down at things nearer,
The moon and pale star,
The deer in the pasture.
All, all things in beauty
Are lovely arrayed,
And as all things please me,
With myself, too, I am pleased.
O fortunate eyes,
Whatever you've seen,   6840
Let it be what it was,
Always lovely it's been.
                              [*Pause.*]

But I've not been posted up here
Only for my own delight—
What is that there, there, that horror,
Glaring in the dark of night?
I see streams of bright sparks pouring
Upward through the linden trees,
Fire ever redder burning,

Fanned to fury by the breeze. 6850
It's the cottage, fiercely blazing,
Damp and mossgrown though it stood—
Help! Help! But it's useless calling
When there's no one by to heed.
How those good old people took
Such care to prevent a fire!
Now they're gasping in its smoke,
What a terrible disaster!
Worse and worse! There's little hope,
Trapped inside the flaming timbers, 6860
The good people can escape
The inferno of hot embers.
Fire licking upward scorches
Leaves and twigs into a flame,
Which, igniting the dry branches,
Brings the great limbs crashing down.
Why must my eyes have to witness
Such things? Have so keen a sight?
There! The chapel now collapses
Under all that crushing weight. 6870
Writhing, darting flames mount higher
To the lindens' very tops
And the hollow trunks, afire,
Crimson glow down to their roots.

[*Long pause, then concluding.*]

What once so pleased our sight
Is swallowed up in time's long night.
FAUST. [*On a balcony overlooking the dunes*]
That mournful strain! It is my watchman
'S grieving song, come tardily.
Oh, I repent me of my action,
It all was done too hastily. 6880
But if the lindens now are only
A charred waste, well, I'll have built
A lookout place from where serenely

I'll contemplate the infinite;
See the house, too, the old couple
Occupy now happily.
There they'll pass their last days, grateful
For my generosity.

MEPHISTO AND THE THREE. [*Speaking from below*]
At top speed we've come running here;
Excuse us, it went badly, sir.   6890
We knocked and banged and knocked again,
Still no one came to let us in.
We shook the old door so hard that
It gave and fell flat at our feet.
We shouted, threatened, cursed till hoarse—
In vain, there was no answering voice.
It's that way always, people don't
Hear a thing because they won't!
So not delaying the least bit,
In we went and cleared them out.   6900
They didn't suffer much, the pair,
Fright carried them off then and there.
A stranger hiding in the place
Put up a fight—for a short space.
In the mêlée embers from
The hearth were scattered round the room;
Some straw ignited and the hot fire
Now makes those three their funeral pyre.

FAUST. You didn't hear a word I said?
I meant a trade, fools, not a raid!   6910
I curse your mindless violence—
The three of you can share my curse!

CHORUS. How they din it in to you:
What the high-ups want, you do!
But when you show your mettle, zeal,
You risk house, home, and neck as well.

                                                [*They go off.*]
FAUST. [*On the balcony*] The stars put out their light, the fire

Dies down, soon it will expire.
I shiver in the cold breeze that
Blows wisps of smoke this way from it.   6920
So quick commanded, done so quick!
—What shapes are these, dim, shadowlike?

MIDNIGHT

Four gray women appear.

THE FIRST. The name I am called by is Lack.
THE SECOND.   Mine is Debt.
THE THIRD. The name I am called by is Care.
THE FOURTH.   Mine is Need.
LACK, DEBT, NEED. The place is locked up, there's no getting in here;
    The fellow is rich so he's not our affair.
LACK. In there I'm a shadow.
DEBT.   I'm nothing, a blank.
NEED. The pampered don't even vouchsafe me a look.
CARE. You mayn't, my sisters, go in, it's denied.
    By the keyhole Care slips without hindrance inside.   6930
                                      [*Care disappears.*]
LACK. It's no place for us here, gray sisters, away!
DEBT. I'll walk by your side, keep you close company.
NEED. And Need follows hard on your heels, nothing loath.
ALL THREE. Clouds race overhead, dim the starry sky's brilliance,
    And behind, speeding here from far off in the distance,
    Who is it I see? Our own brother, yes! Death.
FAUST. [*In the palace*]
    I saw four come, three only went.
    I've no idea what their words meant.
    I thought I heard the word "need," later "loath,"
    Then rhyming mournfully with it came "death."   6940
    It had a muffled, ghostly, hollow note.
    I've still not won my way to freedom yet.
    If only I could leave witchcraft behind me,

Unlearn my spells, put magic by entirely,
And face you, Nature, simply as a man,
It would be worth it being human then—

As I was once, before I tampered with
The things of darkness, cursed the world, myself,
Impiously. Now ghosts so fill the air,
No matter where we turn, right, left, they're there.   6950
The day dawns smiling, rational and bright,
We're tangled in a net of dreams at night.
From green fields we come home contentedly,
A bird croaks: meaning what?—catastrophe!
Bedeviled by superstitions, we imagine
The least thing is a sign, a portent, omen.
And so we tremble, feeling lost, alone.
The door creaks and we stiffen—there's no one.

                                                       [*Stiffens.*]

    —Is someone there?

CARE.   Yes, since you ask, dear Sir.
FAUST. Who are you then?   6960
CARE.   Enough that I am here.
FAUST. [*Enraged*]
    Clear out, you hag!
CARE.   My place is here, where else?
FAUST. [*Mastering his rage, to himself*]
    Remember, you've renounced your magic spells!
CARE.

    Stop your ears so you won't hear me,
    You can't shut your heart against me;
    Taking one shape or another,
    I exert my dire power;
    No matter where, on land, at sea,
    I dog your heels familiarly;
    Never looked for, always found,
    Now placated and now damned—   6970
    Dare to say you've not known Care!

FAUST. I've rushed around the world for many a year,
Chased after everything I fancied, madly,
What didn't satisfy I let go promptly,
On what escaped me didn't waste a tear.
My sole concern has been what?—to desire,
Gain my desire and desire again, all over.
I stormed through life in grand style, mightily,
But wiser now, I act more cautiously.
I've learned enough about the earth we live on;   6980
What lies beyond is closed to human vision.
The man's a fool who, looking up, imagines
There're creatures like himself up in the heavens.
Stand where you are, look round you on the earth,
Our world speaks volumes to a man of worth!
What business has he searching out eternity?
What his eyes show him, that's enough infinity!
Let him live all his earthly days accordingly,
Though ghosts appear he'll wave them off indifferently,
In pressing onwards always, find his joy, his torment,   6990
A being never satisfied, not for one moment!

CARE.

Whom I once get hold of, he will
Find the whole world pointless, futile.
Over him gloom casts its dun net,
Blinding him to sunrise, sunset,
Though possessing all his senses,
Inwardly there's only darkness,
Let him own great heaps of riches,
It's as if they're someone else's,
To him fortune and misfortune   7000
Only are some queer, strange notion,
Although plenty's rich horn over-
Flows for him, he faints from hunger.
Everything he puts off, whether
He likes it or not, till later;
Always waiting, hesitating,

Nothing ever consummating.
FAUST. Enough! You'll get nowhere with me!
    I shut my ears against such rubbish.
    That stupefying litany   7010
    Would make the wisest man turn foolish.
CARE.

       Come or go? He can't decide, he's
       At a loss, he shilly-shallies;
       Straight before him lies the highway,
       Halting, he looks this way, that way.
       More and more confused, he can't see
       Anything as it is clearly,
       Trouble to himself, his neighbor,
       Panting like a driven creature,
       Gasping yet still onwards reeling,   7020
       Obstinately persevering—
       So he goes on on his treadmill,
       Giving up all that's delightful,
       Having to do what he hates, daily,
       Sleeping badly, waking dully,
       Stuck fast where he is until he's
       Ripe for sending down to Hades.
FAUST. Damned specters! This is just what you've done to
    Poor suffering mankind time and time again,
    Turned even the most routine, dull day into   7030
    An ugly nightmare of confusion, pain.
    It's hard, I know, to send our demons packing,
    The bond with them is stringent, who can break it?
    Your power, Care, is great, insidious, cunning,
    Yet I refuse to recognize it!
CARE.

       You do, do you? Well, as I vanish,
       Feel it in my parting curse at last.
       The human race is blind from start to finish:
       Blindness strike you down, too, Faust!

    [*She breathes on him and leaves.*]

FAUST. [*Blinded*]

The night seems darker, presses closer round me,   7040
Yet all is clear, as bright as day, within.
If I'm to get the work done I must hurry,
It needs the Master's voice to move things on.
—Wake up, you fellows, turn to with a good will,
Let me see realized all that I planned.
Get busy now with mattock, pick, and shovel
And make the earth fly in the place you've been assigned!
With discipline and diligence, I promise,
You'll earn yourselves a very handsome bonus.
To get a great work done one mind's   7050
Sufficient for a thousand hands.

GREAT FORECOURT OF THE PALACE

Torches.

MEPHISTO. [*As overseer leading the way*]

Come on, come on, you lemurs, come,
You wambling, shambling creatures!
You makeshift things of skin and bone,
Poor patched up, half-made natures!

LEMURS. [*In chorus*]

At once before you here we stand,
And best as we can grasp it,
What it's about's a lot of land
And we're supposed to get it.

We've brought a stack of sharp stakes here,   7060
Surveyor's chains for measuring;
But why you called us to appear
We've trouble in remembering.

MEPHISTO. It's not an engineering job we've got;
Just use as measure your own length and breadth.
The longest one of you, let him lie flat,
You others mark his outline in the turf,

Then dig a rectilinear hole with the same shape
Was digged for our fathers, longish, deep.
From palace to a narrow room,   7070
That's the stupid end to which things come.

LEMURS. [*Digging with clownish gestures*]
    In youth when I did love, did love,
      Methought it was very sweet!
    From where the reed shrilled, reel spun round,
      I could not keep my feet.

    But stealing age put out his crutch
      And tripped me so I fell flat;
    I stumbled through death's open door—
      Why, why was it not kept shut!

FAUST. [*Coming out of the palace, feeling his way by the doorposts*]
I hear the clink of spades, how happily!   7080
It's my men busy at their digging,
The land and water reconciling
By fixing for the waves their boundary,
Confining in strict bonds the flooding tide.

MEPHISTO. [*Aside*]
Yet your exertions only serve our side:
Those dikes and dams, they're only something good for
The demon Neptune to devour with pleasure.
No matter what you do, it's hopeless,
Your schemes, your energy, all useless;
The elements work with us in close union   7090
Whose end result is death, destruction, ruin.

FAUST. Overseer!

MEPHISTO.   Here!

FAUST.   Use every means
To round up more and more construction gangs.
Encourage them with smiles, drive them with curses,
Pay them, impress them, promise them prizes.
Daily let me have a full report
How far along with the ditch the men have got.

MEPHISTO. [*Under his breath*]
　From the reports I receive,
　It's no ditch, it's a grave.
FAUST. At the foot of the hills there's a fen
　Befouling the great work we've done.　　　　　7100
　To drain that pestilential swamp would be
　My last, my greatest victory!
　It would open up to millions
　Space to work in, build their dwellings;
　If not entirely safe, yet safe enough
　For men to lead a free and active life.
　Fields green and fruitful! Men and herds at ease
　Upon this new-created land, this paradise
　Protected by the massive, mighty barrier
　A fearless people raised by their hard labor!　　　7110
　A veritable Eden here inside,
　Although the flood foam at the brink outside!
　If a crack appearing, the sea pours in, then each
　By common impulse race to repair the breach.
　Yes, I believe, uphold as my fixed faith,
　As the ultimate truth we human beings know:
　He only earns his freedom, life itself,
　Who daily strives to conquer it anew.
　So, so we'd pass, amid the dangers here,
　As child, grown man, and graybeard, the busy year.　7120
　To see such life, such glad activity!
　To stand with free men upon ground that's free!
　Then, then, I might say to the passing moment,
　"Linger awhile, you are so fair!
　The footprints of my earthly passage cannot
　Even after eons disappear."
　Foreseeing such scenes of unmatched contentment,
　I now enjoy the highest, supreme moment.

　[*Faust collapses; the Lemurs catch him and lay him on the
ground.*]

MEPHISTO. No pleasure was enough for him, no happiness,
Forever running after this, that, anything.   7130
And the poor wretch, imagine, wants to cling
To this last moment, empty, meaningless.
Mightily he withstood me, I allow,
But time the master has laid the old man low.
His clock has stopped—
CHORUS.   Yes, still as midnight, silenced!
The hands drop off—
MEPHISTO.   Drop off, and all is finished.
CHORUS. Over, done!
MEPHISTO.   That's stupid—*over, done!*
What's been and what has never been—they're one,
The same! What point is there in all of this creating
When back created things are dragged to nothing?   7140
"It's over, done!" Really, what does that mean?
It means it just as well might not have been.
Yet round and round it goes, convinced it's real!
For me eternal emptiness has more appeal.

BURIAL

LEMUR. [*Solo*]
Who built this house, so illy made
With a rude spade and shovel?
LEMURS. [*Chorus*]
For you, lank guest, in burlap dressed,
It's good enough, it's ample.
LEMUR. [*Solo*]
Who furnished it? So bare the place,
No table, chair, nor bedstead.   7150
LEMURS. [*Chorus*]
Its things were had on a short lease,
Time ran, the lease expired.
MEPHISTO. Here's the body, if the soul should try
Eluding me, I will instantly whip out

The bond he signed in blood. Alas, today
There are so many ways by which to cheat
The Devil of his due. Things tried and true,
Our ancient practice and procedure,
Is frowned upon, and our new
Has not, it seemed, found overwhelming favor.   7160
I could have managed things all by myself once;
These days I need to send down for assistance.

No, it's a bad time now for us.
Old customs, ancient rights in us invested
You can't rely on! Once it was the case,
The last breath breathed, why then the soul departed.
I watched and waited like a cat,
Then pounced with claws extended—caught!
But now it hesitates, it hangs back, nervous,
And doesn't want to leave the loathsome carcass,   7170
Whose elements, in fierce war with each other,
Finally force it to make an ignoble departure.
Day and night I'm plagued, not knowing where
Or when or how the damned thing will appear.
Death's grown feeble, lost his old dispatch.
Has he even come, you wonder anxiously;
I've often watched the stiffened members greedily—
Deceived! Again the body stirs, limbs stretch.

[*Conjuring with fantastic, troop-leader gestures.*]

Come on, step lively, rally here to me,
You straight- and crook-horned lords of the dark below,   7180
You devils of the old, true pedigree,
And bring the jaws of Hell along with you!
It has a lot of jaws, Hell, needless to relate,
For swallowing souls according to their standing;
From now on, though, we shan't differentiate:
All's liberal now and so must be man's ending.
          [*Hell's jaws yawn horridly on the left.*]

The tusks unclose, from the gaping gullet
A raging flood of flames pours out furiously,
And in the boiling clouds of smoke behind it
I see the Fiery City, burning eternally.   7190
The red surge beats right up against the teeth,
The damned swim up it, desperate to escape,
The huge hyena jaws close with a snap,
And once again they flounder in the surf.
There's lots more going on, too, in the corners—
The horrors crammed inside so little room!
You're right to terrify the stubborn sinners
Who still think it's illusion, a bad dream.

[*To the fat devils with short, straight horns.*]

You demons with your great guts, flaming cheeks,
How your fat shines with the true sulfurous sweat!   7200
You blocks, you stumps, with short, unmoving necks,
Look, do you see a phosphorescent glint?
Know that's winged Psyche, that's the little soul:
Pluck off its wings, what is it, just a worm!
When it creeps out, I'll stamp it with my seal,
Then down with it into Hell's hot maelstrom!

Your duty, fat fiends, is to mount
A guard upon the lower region.
Whether the soul has its preferred resort
Below the waistline, no one can be certain,   7210
But in the navel it feels right at home—
Take care or whish! right past you it will zoom.

[*To the lanky devils with long, crooked horns.*]

You clowns who sway on thin shanks, giantlike,
Reach up and with your sharp claws rake
The air above, about him, keep right at it
So as to catch the fluttering, fleeting spirit!

In its decaying old house, I will bet,
It's not so pleasant, soon it must fly out.

[*Burst of light from above right.*]

THE HEAVENLY HOST.
    Fly, angels, winging
    Unhurriedly, bringing   7220
    Sinners in darkness
    Blessed forgiveness,
    Dust restoring to life!
    With loving-kindness
    Staying your passing,
    For all natures tracing
    The celestial path!

MEPHISTO. What jarring, jangling tones those are I hear,
    Accompanying that unwelcome glare!
    The sort of inept, unsexed, shrill falsetto   7230
    The godly's pious, sniveling taste delights so.
    You know how in our wickedest hour we sought
    To cut off humankind right at the root—
    Well, the most awful thing we could devise
    Is just what in their piety they prize.

    Hymn-singing here they come, the frauds, so unctuous!
    They steal souls from us, lie, cheat, plagiarize
    Our own methods which they use against us:
    They're devils, too, but wearing a disguise.
    Let them win here, your shame will know no end,   7240
    So stand fast round the graveside, every fiend!

CHORUS OF ANGELS. [*Scattering roses*]
    Roses that dazzling show,
    Roses that crimson glow,
    The air perfuming
    With life-giving balm!
    Fluttering, hovering,
    As if, leaf-winged, flying—

Your petals unfolding,
Burst into bloom!

Appear now, appear, Spring,   7250
In red and green dressed,
Paradisiac joys bring
To him here at rest!

MEPHISTO. [*To the devils*]

You duck, you flinch! Is that what devils do?
Get back, fools, into your places!
Never mind them and their roses!
It's plain to see the angels mean to snow
You hot fellows under cool, pink drifts,
But your foul breath makes rose-falls melt and dwindle,
So blow hard each and every devil!   7260
—Enough! The swarm of petals, fading, wilts.
Go easy! Clap your mouths and noses shut!
It's too hard, too hot, all your huffing, puffing;
You're so infernally immoderate!
The stuff's not only dried up, it is burning,
And drifts down on us as bright, stinging sparks—
Hold steady, never waver, close up ranks!
—Their courage fails them, gone from them's their strength,
The devils feel a strange, seductive warmth.

CHORUS OF ANGELS.

Blessed blooms shower   7270
Love all around,
Dancing flames scatter
Joys without end,
All that hearts wish for—
Like words of truth burning
Bright in the sky,
For all our host making
Eternal day!

MEPHISTO. Oh damn those dolts, befuddled, woozy!

The lot of them knocked topsy-turvy,   7280
They backward somersault and tumble
Tail first down to Hell, each devil.
Enjoy your steambath which you well deserve!
But as for me, I'm here and I won't move.

[*Flailing his arms wildly to repel the roses.*]

Away, false lights, for all your brilliancy
What are you, caught?—nasty, jellyish matter.
Go flutter somewhere else and let me be!
—They stick to my neck, burn like pitch and sulfur.

CHORUS OF ANGELS.
 What isn't your affair,
 You must avoid it!   7290
 Guard, each, your soul from care,
 Never endure it!
 We must, when hard beset,
 Answer back harder yet.
 Love only lovers shows
 Where the way lies.

MEPHISTO. My head, my heart, my liver, they burn so!
 It's superdiabolical, this power,
 Much sharper, fiercer, hotter than Hellfire,
 Oh it beats anything below!   7300
 So this is why the despised lover
 Screws his neck round to spy out
 The least sign of his sweetheart—

 As I do, too! Why should my heard be turned
 By enemies that I have always scorned,
 The sight of whom used to arouse my fury?
 What thing's got hold of me, what unknown force,
 So that I'm tongue-tied, can no longer curse,
 And look with longing at boys who are pretty?
 If I'm made a damned fool of, in my folly,   7310

I'll be called fool forever, don't I know it!
And though my hatred for them has no limit,
They seem, the imps, so tempting, teasing, lovely!

You darling children, isn't it quite true
We're all of us the sons of Lucifer?
I'd like to kiss each pretty one of you!
Just at the right time, it seems, here you are—
So natural it feels, no strain or fuss,
As if we'd passed many an hour together.
So sly you are, tomcat-ish, lecherous: 7320
Each time I look at you you're looking better.
Come nearer, let me have a closer look!

CHORUS OF ANGELS. We're coming, yes, but why do you draw back?
Stay where you are, unflinching, if you're able.

[*The angels, filling up the stage, force Mephistopheles to the front.*]

MEPHISTO. Spirits damned we are, you say,
But you are the real witchery,
Indifferently seducing male and female.
—What a dismal, damnable affair!
Call this the right romantic atmosphere?
My whole body's in a sweat, a fever,   7330
I hardly notice how my burned neck pains me!
—You flutter this way, that way: come down lower
And swing those hips a little more profanely.
It suits you fine, your gravity,
But do smile once, just once, at me.
How I would be delighted by it—
I mean the way that lovers do it—
A softening around the mouth, no more!
You tall one, I like you the best, beshrew me!
That priestly air detracts from your allure;   7340
Do look at me, please, just a little lewdly!
Also, that long shirt's much too modest for you;
You're overdressed, more nudity's more fitting.

—Around they turn and offer me a rear view!
Oh those young scamps are simply too, too fetching!

CHORUS OF ANGELS.

Clearer and clearer burn,
Each loving flame!
On all the sinful turn
Your saving beam,
Truth by its brightness heal   7350
All who themselves condemn,
Having done ill,
So that, redeemed at last,
With all the blest they're blest!

MEPHISTO. [*Getting a grip on himself*]

What's happened to me? —Joblike I've been struck
From head to foot with boils so that I shudder
To see myself. Yet still when I look deeper
Into myself—unbeaten! trusting ever
In my descent from Hell's old, hardy stock:
The Devil's parts still full of pith and might,   7360
He's got a rash, that's all, from his love-fit.
The horrid flames have burnt down, flicker out.
And as the Devil should: I curse you, the whole lot!

CHORUS OF ANGELS.

Whom, holy fire,
You hover over
Find at last life has
Goodliness, blitheness.
Together all rise,
Loudly give praise!
Air now blows purely   7370
Soul can breathe freely!

[*They rise upward, bearing off Faust's immortal part.*]

MEPHISTO. [*Looking around*]

What's happened? —All gone, disappeared, they have!
You youngsters caught me, you did, off my guard

And flew off with the booty heavenward!
So that's why they were hanging round this grave.
I've lost a rare prize, long looked for reward;
From under my nose they stole craftily
The great soul that was pledged me solemnly.

And where is there a court I can appeal to,
Restore to me what I'm owed rightfully?   7380
In my old age to let myself be fooled so—
And who's to blame for the fiasco, me!
Oh, I have made a mess of things, I have;
All that great effort simply thrown away,
And why? A vulgar itch, absurd desire—love!—
Which turned the tough old Devil shamefully
Into a poor milksop. For me to carry
On like that, the shrewd, all-knowing Fiend,
Shows it was no small thing, the childish folly
That got the better of me in the end.   7390

MOUNTAIN RAVINES

A wilderness of forest and rock, with holy anchorites living in clefts up and down the mountainside.

CHORUS AND ECHO.
Woods sway and lean toward us,
Cliffs beetle over us,
Roots clutch crags in their grip,
Trees crowd the stony slope.
Cascades pour down in waves,
For shelter there are caves.
Lions forget to growl,
Like tame cats round us prowl,
Honoring this sacred seat,
Heavenly love's retreat.   7400

PATER ECSTATICUS. [*Floating up and down above the ground*]
Fire of endless bliss,
Love's searing spirit-kiss,
Heart filled with scalding blood,
God-joy a foaming flood!
Arrows, transfix this flesh,
Lances, defeat this flesh,
Clubs, fall and smash this flesh,
Lightnings, make ash this flesh,
Till all things valueless
Dwindle to nothingness   7410
And the pure love alone
Starlike forever burn!
PATER PROFUNDUS. [*Far below*]
The chasm at my feet, dark, yawning,
Rests on a chasm deeper still,
A thousand streams, their waters joining,
In a cascade terrific fall;
The tree's own life, its strength from nature,
Its trunk lifts skyward straight and tall—
All, all, show love's almighty power
That shapes all things, cares for them all.   7420

The storm breaks round me, fiercely howling,
The woods, ravines, all seem to quake,
And yet, swelled by the deluge falling,
The torrent plunges down the rock
To water lovingly the valley;
The lightning burns the overcast
And clears the air, now smelling freshly,
Of all its foulness, dankness, mist—

All love proclaim! the creative power
By which the whole world is embraced.   7430
Oh kindle, too, in me your fire,

Whose thoughts, disordered, cold, depressed,
Inside the cage of dull sense languish,
Tormented, helpless, hard beset!
Dear God, relieve my spirit's anguish,
My needy heart illuminate!

PATER SERAPHICUS. [*Midway up*]
What, a rosy dawn cloud is it,
There above that pine's fringed crown?
I believe I know what's in it:
Souls upgathered when just born.   7440

CHORUS OF BOY SOULS.
Where, where will it end, our journey?
Tell us, Father, who we are.
Our existence is so happy,
Weighs on us as light as air.

PATER SERAPHICUS.
Boys born at the stroke of midnight,
Snatched away as life began;
For their parents a sad forfeit,
For the angel host, pure gain.
—You can feel love's presence near you,
Venture closer, nothing fear;   7450
Life's hard ways have never scarred you,
Lucky spirits that you are!
Children, come and enter into
My old earth-accustomed eyes;
Through them you can look about you,
View the world that round you lies.

[*He takes them into himself.*]

These are trees, these precipices,
Over which with awful force
Water in a torrent rushes,
Shortening its downward course.   7460

BOY SOULS. [*From inside*]
Yes, a scene sublime, impressive,

Much too gloomy we think, though;
Makes us tremble, apprehensive—
Noble, good Sir, let us go!

PATER SERAPHICUS.

Higher rise, still higher, growing
Stronger imperceptibly,
Near the Divine Presence gaining
A more perfect purity!
What is it the spirit thrives on,
What fills the ethereal space?   7470
Endless love whose revelation
Blitheness brings, eternal bliss.

BOY SOULS. [*Circling the highest peaks*]

All join hands, turning
Round in a ring!
Your voices raising,
Holily sing!
Divinely schooled at last,
You can feel sure
You will behold at last
Whom you revere.   7480

ANGELS. [*Hovering in the upper air, carrying Faust's immortal part*]

He's saved from evil, the great soul,
Confounding clever Satan:
"Who strives, and keeps on striving still,
For him there is redemption!"
And if love, pinnacled on high,
Has also watched out for him,
The angelic legions of the sky
Will fly round him in welcome.

THE YOUNGER ANGELS.

With the roses we were given
By much-loving, holy women—   7490
Penitents—we won the battle
For this soul against the Devil:
Our great work is now completed.

Taking to their heels, the wicked
Spirits scattered when we pelted
Them with rosebuds: not their wonted
Hellish torments but the tortured
Anguish love inflicts, they suffered.
Even their old captain, Satan,
Winced to feel himself love-smitten.   7500
We've prevailed! Exult, all Heaven!

THE MORE PERFECT ANGELS.

This human scrap, we find,
'S painful to carry,
Even if bleached and burned,
Still impure, earthy.
Once spirit has been joined
Fast to gross nature,
Parting them, that are wound
So close together,
Is something far above   7510
Angelic power:
Only Eternal Love
Can do that ever.

THE YOUNGER ANGELS.

All round that rocky height
Cloudlets are sailing:
Can they be spirits that
My eyes are seeing?
Yes, it's becoming clear,
I see a troop appear
Of blessed children,   7520
Who, freed from earth's sore weight,
Turn in a ring,
Uplifted with delight
In the new spring
Weather of Heaven.
Let him begin with them
Upwards to mount,

Rise with them, reach with them
The crowning height.

BOY SOULS.

We welcome gladly   7530
This new, unfledged soul!
The angels' assurance
Embraces us all.
All earthly remnants
Strip away from him—
Look, look, how lovely
Holiness makes him!

DOCTOR MARIANUS. [*In the highest, barest, purest cell*]

Here nothing blocks the view,
The mind's uplifted.
Women float skywards, to   7540
Heaven exalted.
In their midst, glorious,
The Queen of Heaven,
Star-crowned, victorious,
Sublimest woman.

[*Ecstatically.*]

Under the stretched tent of sky,
Empress, Mother, Virgin,
Let me view your mystery,
Grant my eyes such vision!
Solemn, tender feelings move   7550
In my man's breast for you,
Don't, oh don't refuse the love
That I offer to you.

Our courage nothing daunts,
By your glory summoned,
Milder burn our zealous hearts,
By your pity softened.
Purest maid that's ever been!
Womanhood's example!

This world's Mistress, chosen Queen!   7560
The gods' peer and equal!

Small clouds float round her
In the blue heaven:
Penitents they are,
Too-loving women,
Breathing the ether
Round her and, kneeling,
For grace appealing.

Spotless as you are, unsmirched,
Yet it's been allowed you   7570
That the easily seduced,
Trusting, should turn to you.

How should they, compliant, weak,
Not yield to temptation?
Who by his own strength can break
Out of lust's close prison?
On slippery ground how easily
The foot meets with mischances,
Who's not seduced by flattery,
By amorous sighs and glances?   7580

[*The Mater Gloriosa floats by.*]

CHORUS OF PENITENTS.
As up to Heaven
You pass, Mary, listen,
Hear our petition!
Lady beyond compare,
Full of grace, hear, O hear!
MAGNA PECCATRIX. [*Luke 7:36*]
By the dear love which, defiant
Of the Pharisee's derision,
Bathed your son's feet in its fragrant

Balsam tears as in a fountain,
By the jar which generously   7590
Dripped sweet-smelling unction on them,
By the hair which rapturously
Rubbed his sacred limbs to dry them—

MULIER SAMARITANA. [*John 4*]
By the well where Abraham led
Flocks of sheep and goats to water,
By the pail which, when he thirsted,
Cooled the lips of our Savior,
By the streams of living water
Pouring out from that pure fountain
Prodigally and forever,   7600
Flowing through all of creation—

MARIA AEGYPTIACA. [*Acta Sanctorum*]
By the sacred place in which they
Laid our Lord to rest in earth,
By the unseen arm that pushed me
From the door and warned me off,
By the forty years I dwelt in
Desert wastes, my sins atoned,
By the blessed farewell written
With my finger in the sand—

ALL THREE.
You who never turn away from   7610
Sinners overwhelmed by scandal,
Who the comfort penance brings them
Augment into bliss eternal,
Pardon, too, this girl who only
Fell once, hardly conscious of it,
Lavish on her your sweet mercy,
Surely, good soul, she deserves it!

ONE OF THE PENITENTS. [*Formerly called Gretchen, pressing up to her*]
Look, Lady without peer,
Shining resplendently,
Down at me happily   7620

Kneeling here,
Look!
He's been restored to me
Him I adored, now free,
He has come back!

BOY SOULS. [*Circling nearer*]
He's bigger grown, stronger than
We are, already,
For our faithful care of him,
We'll be repaid amply.
How soon in our innocence   7630
Death came to snatch us,
But with his experience,
How much he can teach us.

THE PENITENT. [*Gretchen*]
A novice in the spirit chorus,
His newborn self he hardly knows:
How renewed life within him courses,
How soon one of the blessed he grows.
See how the last threads still attaching
His striving spirit to the earth
He breaks, and clad in celestial clothing   7640
Appears in all of youth's first strength!
Oh let me, Mary, be his teacher,
He's dazzled still in the new dawn!

MATER GLORIOSA.
Rise up to higher spheres and higher!
With you before, he'll follow. Come.

DOCTOR MARIANUS. [*Fallen on his face in adoration*]
Look up, chastened, contrite hearts,
To those saving features,
Know the blessing that awaits
All transfigured natures!
Every better purpose turn   7650
To her sacred service!

—Be, O Virgin, Mother, Queen,
Goddess, to us gracious!

CHORUS MYSTICUS.

All things ephemeral
Are symbols only,
The inaccessible
Here is known finally,
The inexpressible
Here's acted, done;
The eternal feminine   7660
Beckons us on.

Finis

NOTES

ACT I

Page (line)

1 (17) *Lethe river.* In Hades. Drinking its water gave forgetfulness.

5 (120) *Junker.* Young nobleman.

8 (235) *Guelph and Ghibelline.* The two warring "parties" of the early middle ages, the first supporting the pope, the second the German emperor.

9 (259) *Jew.* Moneylender. As a pariah people of Christian Europe, the pariah occupation of moneylending was unbenevolently allowed Jews.

11 (345) *The sun's pure gold.* In astrological lore, each planet (sun and moon being thought planets) had an associated metal.. Mercury's was quicksilver, the moon's silver, Saturn's lead.

11 (348) *early and late.* Venus shines as the morning and evening star.

11 (359) *the learned man.* Mephistopheles is recommending the services of Faust.

12 (369) *mandrakes.* Herbs superstitiously credited with all kinds of powers.

14 (460) *Death the Master.* The translation borrows from Paul Celan, "Der Tod ist ein Meister aus Deutschland."

17 (530) *Theophrastus.* Greek philosopher of the late fourth–early third centuries B.C. whose writings on plants are regarded as the first systematic botany.

20 (611) *Punchinellos.* Clowns in the commedia dell'arte, the once traditional Italian farce.

20 (630) *Parasites.* Hangers-on of the rich in ancient comedy.

22 (689) *Night and Graveyard poets.* The first sort dealt in Gothic horrors, the second in meditations on human mortality. These were eighteenth-century English literary fashions that crossed over to the Continent in the nineteenth.

22 (689) *Graces.* Goddesses who lent social life agreeableness and grace.

23 (695) *Fates.* The goddess Clotho spins the thread of life, Lachesis decides its length, Atropos cuts it off. Of course Atropos is much complained about, so in keeping with the holiday spirit the kindlier Clotho changes places with her.

24 (740) *Furies.* Avenging spirits, here changed from the hags of tragedy into fomenters of marital strife and punishers of infidelity.

25 (769) *Asmodeus.* In Jewish demonology also a fomenter of strife.

28 (847) *Zoilo-Thersites.* Mephistopheles disguised. The name combines those of

247

two vituperators of classical times: Zoilus, a philosopher famous for his railing against Homer, and Thersites, the foul-mouthed railer in the *Iliad* against the Greek army's leaders.

29 (915) *Boy Charioteer.* The personification of poetry, reappearing in Act III as Euphorion, child of Faust and Helen.

31 (965) *Plutus.* Faust, playing the part of the god of wealth.

33 (1045) *Skin-and-Bones.* Mephisto again.

38 (1203) *Pan.* The Emperor as the god of All. "Pan" was understood by a common etymological misinterpretation to mean "all."

40 (1264) *three commandments.* Those against theft, adultery, and killing.

44 (1402) *salamanders.* Mythical creatures able to live in fire.

44 (1424) *Nereids.* Daughters of the sea god Nereus, one of whom, Thetis, was won in marriage by a mortal, Peleus, by whom she had Achilles.

52 (1668) *Frenchman's fable.* The Frenchman is the great seventeenth-century fabulist La Fontaine.

58 (1877) *Paris.* The Trojan prince whose abduction to Troy of Helen, wife of the Spartan king Menelaus, brought about the siege of Troy. He had grown up as a shepherd on Mount Ida.

59 (1920) *That lovely form.* See *Part One,* lines 2469–80.

60 (1935) *Luna and Endymion.* The moon goddess, smitten by the beauty of Endymion, descended from the skies to steal a kiss from the sleeping youth.

60 (1956) *At ten already.* Theseus stole Helen when she was ten years old.

61 (1964) *She always pleased Troy's ancients.* The elders of Troy, seeing Helen below from the walls, exclaim:

> We cannot rage at her, it is no wonder
> that Trojans and Akhaians under arms
> should for so long have borne the pains of war
> for one like this.—*Iliad,* Book III (Fitzgerald translation)

ACT II

64 (2048) *Famulus.* Academic assistant.

64 (2063) *Oremus!* "Let us pray!"—to ward off evil spirits.

(2072) Dr. Wagner. Faust's old famulus in *Part One.*

66 (2117) *A B.A. now.* The freshman looking for advice about his studies in the scene Faust's Study (II), in *Part One.*

72 (2311) *Homunculus.* Little man.

73 (2343) *But one stands out.* Leda, whom Jupiter, taking a swan's shape, possessed, from which union sprang Helen and the twins Castor and Pollux, called the Dioscuri.

74 (2391) *Peneios.* A river that flows through Thessaly to empty into the Aegean.

74 (2393) *Pharsalus.* On the plain below the town of Pharsalus, Caesar triumphed over Pompey in 48 B.C.

76 (2444) *Erichtho.* A Thessalian witch described by the Roman poet Lucan in his *Pharsalia,* an epic poem on the war between Caesar and Pompey.

79 (2526) *Antaeus-like.* Like the giant who drew his strength from contact with the earth.

79 (2539) *modern style.* The nineteenth century turned prudish in recoil from the immodesties of the eighteenth.

80 (2562) *Arimaspians.* A fabulous people who tried to steal the treasure traditionally guarded by the griffins.

81 (2605) *Sirens.* Half bird, half woman, they sang sailors to their destruction.

82 (2640) *Ulysses.* Curious to hear the sirens' song, he had himself

> lashed to the mast,
>
> and if I shout and beg to be untied,
>
> take more turns of the rope to muffle me.
>
> —*Odyssey,* XII (Fitzgerald translation)

83 (2653) *Chiron.* A centaur, the wise and kindly tutor of heroes.

83 (2674) *Stymphalides.* Monstrous birds whom Hercules destroyed as one of his twelve labors.

84 (2684) *Lernaean Hydra.* Another of Hercules' labors was to exterminate the many-headed serpent of the Lernaean swamp.

84 (2694) *Lamiae.* Female demons who lusted after human flesh and blood.

85 (2735) *once before I knew such joy.* When he dreamt of Leda and the swan, as reported by Homunculus (p. 73).

87 (2801) *Argonauts.* Heroes named after their ship, the Argo, in which they sailed in search of the Golden Fleece.

87 (2805) *Mentor,* Telemachus's teacher, whose shape Pallas Athena assumes in the *Odyssey.*

88 (2834) *Boreads.* Winged sons of the north wind, Boreas.

89 (2855) *Hebe.* Goddess of youth and wife to Hercules after he was made immortal.

90 (2903) *Pherae.* A story about Achilles unites him and Helen, after their deaths, as lovers on the island of Leuce, which name Goethe replaced with that of the Thessalian town of Pherae.

90 (2917) *Manto.* A Sibyl or prophetess whom Goethe makes the daughter of Aesculapius, the physician god.

91 (2936) *greatest realm.* The Macedonian empire, defeated by republican Rome in 168 B.C. at Pydna (which lies north of Olympus, in Macedonia, not south).

93 (2990) *Seismos.* The earthquake personified.

93 (3006) *Latona* (Leto). When she was big with Apollo and Diana by Jupiter, Neptune raised up Delos as a refuge for her from Juno's anger. Goethe substitutes Seismos for Neptune.

96 (3094) *Dactyls.* Legendary tiny creatures (*daktyl* means "finger" in Greek).

97 (3134) *The Cranes of Ibycus.* Cranes were traditional enemies of the pygmies. In a ballad by Schiller they avenge the murder of the poet Ibycus.

 98 (3154) *Blocksberg region.* The region of the Brocken where the witches celebrate Walpurgis Night in *Part One.* Ilse (*Ilsenstein*), Heinrich (*Heinrichshöhe*),
the Schnarchers ("snorers") are rock formations; Elend ("misery") is a poor
village.

 99 (3208) *Empusa.* A demon of many shapes.

101 (3254) *thryrsus.* The staff carried by the maenads, fierce female followers of
Dionysus.

102 (3288) *Oread.* A mountain nymph.

103 (3329) *Anaxagoras, Thales.* Early Greek philosophers whom Goethe makes
represent the opposing sides of a contemporary geological controversy between the so-called Vulcanists and Neptunists. The Vulcanist Anaxagoras
attributes the origin and progress of life to fiery explosions and sudden con-
vulsions. The Neptunist Thales sees life arising out of water and advancing by
steady, patient evolution.

104 (3351) *myrmidons.* Here, ants.

105 (3401) *huge and menacing sphere.* Anaxagoras mistakes a meteor for the moon.

106 (3443) *Dryad.* A tree nymph.

107 (3451) *Phorkyads.* Gray-haired from birth, they personify ugly old age. Also
called the Graiae.

107 (3473) *Ops and Rhea.* Ops (Roman), the wife of Saturn; Rhea (Greek), the
wife of Cronos.

107 (3474) *The Parcae.* The Fates.

109 (3534) *Nereids and Tritons.* For the Nereids, see note to p. 44. The Tritons were
fish-tailed sons of Neptune.

110 (3566) *Cabiri.* Primitive deities whose obscure mystery cult was centered in
Samothrace. Like Castor and Pollux, rescuers of shipwrecked sailors.

112 (3632) *Dorids.* Also daughters of Nereus, named however after their mother,
the nymph Doris.

112 (3639) *Galatea.* Nereus's best-loved daughter, here described as the successor
to foam-born Venus on Cyprus.

112 (3644) *Paphos.* A Cyprian city.

112 (3645) *chariot throne.* Aphrodite's "scallop shell" (line 3640).

113 (3649) *Proteus.* Another ancient sea god, famous for his quick changes.

113 (3669) *Chelone's giant shell.* Chelone was a nymph whom Mercury changed to
a tortoise.

114 (3697) *the eighth's there that / Nobody's thought of yet.* Goethe is mocking the
speculations of contemporary scholarship about the little known Cabiri.

117 (3775) *Telchines.* A legendary race of Rhodes. Skilled smiths, they were credited with forging Neptune's trident and erecting the Rhodian Colossus and
many other bronze statues.

117 (3775) *hippocamps.* Sea horses.

117 (3787) *Helios.* The sun god.

120 (3866) *Psilli and Marsi.* Names of primitive races that Goethe appropriated for his nymphs that guard Venus's sea car.

120 (3882) *Eagle and Winged Lion, Crucifix and Crescent.* Romans and Venetians, Crusaders and Turks, all rulers of Cyprus at one time or another.

ACT III

125 (4005) *Eurus.* The east wind.

125 (4010) *Tyndareus.* Husband of Leda, Helen's mother. The children of Leda and Tyndareus were Clytemnestra, Helen, and Castor and Pollux, the last three fathered by the Jovian swan. (See note to p. 73.)

125 (4012) *Pallas's hill.* A hill on which stood a temple to Pallas Athena.

126 (4029) *shrine on Cythera.* The temple of Venus on Cythera, a Mediterranean island off the southern Peloponnesus.

126 (4061) *Eurotas's waters.* Sparta, on the river Eurotas, lay upstream of where it flows into the sea.

131 (4212) *Phorkyas.* Mephistopheles, disguised as a Phorkyad.

134 (4333) *Erebus.* Undermost part of the underworld.
Mother Night. Out of Chaos and Old Night the world was born.

135 (4339) *Orion.* Giant hunter changed into a constellation at his death.

135 (4340) *Harpies.* Monstrous bird-women who fouled food with their excrement.

135 (4362) *Orcus.* Hades.

136 (4386) *Patroclus, Pelides.* Patroclus is Achilles' (Pelides') close comrade in the *Iliad.*

136 (4405) *two of you were seen . . . in Ilium . . . in Egypt.* A post-Homeric legend has Paris abducting a phantom Helen to Troy, while Mercury saves the real one by carrying her off to Egypt.

137 (4409) *Achilles rose up from / The empty shadow world.* See note to p. 90.

137 (4420) *three-headed dog's jaws.* Hell's watchdog Cerberus.

141 (4545) *bloodthirsty.* Achilles, to Hector fallen in the dust:
> Would god my passion drove me
> to slaughter you and eat you raw.
> —*Iliad*, XXII (Fitzgerald translation)

144 (4638) *Hermes* (Mercury). Conductor of dead souls to Hades.

145 (4657) *Pythoness.* Prophetess, witch.

146 (4687) *bitter ashes.* The apples of Sodom, fair appearing but proving otherwise when bitten. See *Paradise Lost*, X, 564– 66.

148 (4776) *simply one.* The first Helen.—*two of me.* The Helen in Troy and Egypt at the same time (see note to p. 136).—*three . . . four.* The third and fourth Helens are the one come back to Sparta and the one now translated to Faust's medieval castle.

155 (4976) *Nestor.* Oldest of the Greek captains who fought at Troy, ruler of Messenian Pylos.

157 (5038) *broken shell.* Swan-begotten Helen was born from an egg.

159 (5089) *Arcadia.* A region in the Peloponnesus that Virgil established in poetic tradition as the ideal place of pastoral peace and beauty.

160 (5118) *a boy jumping.* Euphorion. See note to p. 29.

162 (5160) *Maia's son.* Hermes.

168 (5339) *The watchword's war.* An allusion to the Greek war of independence against the Turks in the 1820s and to Byron's efforts in that struggle.

170 (5404) *well-known figure.* Byron, here associated with Euphorion as the spirit of poetry and memorialized in the elegiacal stanzas that follow.

173 (5474) *Inscrutable Ones.* Pluto and Proserpine, king and queen of the Underworld.

175 (5537) *Silenus.* The infant Bacchus's nurse, later his drinking companion, traditionally mounted on a donkey.

ACT IV

179 (5606) *Eph. 6:12.* The "wicked spirits," once confined below in darkness, now occupy the "high places," the airy heavens: they have come up in the world.

179 (5620) *Moloch.* In the Bible, a fearsome pagan god; later, as in Milton, one of Satan's crew.

179 (5634) *the Devil's Rock, the Devil's Bridge.* Striking rock formations, so named by popular superstition.

186 (5845) *English play. A Midsummer Night's Dream.*

195 (6124) *little flames.* Saint Elmo's fire, the flames (or fireballs) seen on ships' spars in storms, called Castor and Pollux by the Romans. They light up the spear tips, Faust says, as the last effort of that fading pair of gods.

195 (6135) *necromancer.* The Sabine sorcerer of p. 189.

197 (6194) *my two grim ravens.* Messengers of Wotan (Odin) in the Teutonic mythology, they were reassigned to the Devil by Christian superstition.

198 (6248) *Undines.* Water sprites.

ACT V

210 (6596/6606) *Baucis, Philemon.* The pious, god-fearing couple of one of Ovid's stories in his *Metamorphoses.* The classical names ring incongruously here.

225 (7056) *Lemurs.* For the Romans, malignant specters of the dead still possessing skeletons and shreds of skin and sinew. Goethe shows them as oafs.

226 (7072) *In youth when I did love.* Compare the Gravedigger's song in *Hamlet* V.i.

227 (7124) "Linger awhile, you are so fair." See *Part One,* line 1718.

228 (7145) *Who built this house.* Compare the third stanza of the Gravedigger's song in *Hamlet,* V.i.

230 (7203) *Psyche.* Greek for "soul," usually represented with the wings of a butterfly.

231 (7235) *Is just what in their piety they prize.* The churches prized the soprano voices of castrati for their choirs.

236 (7390) *anchorites.* The fathers Ecstaticus, Profundus, Seraphicus, and Marianus who speak below—holy men retired into the wilderness utterly to devote themselves to the divine love; Doctor Marianus to Mary, Glorious Mother, especially.

239 (7483) *"Who strives, and keeps on striving still / For him there is redemption!"* Goethe emphasized these lines by putting quotation marks around them (they are not a quotation). To J. P. Eckermann, his Boswell, he said they hold "the key to Faust's salvation." Coleridge appended a moral to *The Ancient Mariner* ("He prayeth best who loveth best," etc.), feeling that so shadowy a poem required some moral illumination however feeble. In much the same way, Goethe seems to have felt that *Faust* needed a clearly marked moral to illuminate its obscurity.

242 (7586) *Magna Peccatrix.* The woman who sinned greatly in Luke 7:36–50.

243 (7594) *Mulier Samaritana.* The Samaritan woman with five husbands in John 4:7–26.

243 (7602) *Maria Aegyptiaca. (Acta Sanctorum).* Mary of Egypt, also a repentant sinner, whose story is told in the *Acts of the Saints* (April 2), a Catholic calendar of the lives of saints.

JOHANN WOLFGANG VON GOETHE

Faust

PART TWO

Translated from the German by Martin Greenberg

Goethe's *Faust, Part Two* is distinguished by its extraordinary range of allusion, tone, and style. Full of variety of historical scene and poetic effect, the masterpiece is at times satirical, witty, and even broadly comic, at others grand and soaring. This sparkling new translation of *Faust, Part Two* now affords English-language readers much of the pleasure afforded readers of the original German. Award-winning translator Martin Greenberg casts Goethe's verse in a natural, vigorous, lucid English that preserves Goethe's poetic effects while accurately rendering the sense of the original lines.

The book contains a preface by the translator that helps to bridge the abrupt transition from Part One to Part Two. The story is still that of Faust and his compact with Mephistopheles, but no longer narrowly domestic, ranging through classical Greece, medieval and modern Europe, and an exalted conclusion in a Goethean heaven.

Martin Greenberg is the recipient of a citation from the American Academy and Institute of Arts and Letters for versatility, skill, and probity as both critic and translator. He has also received the Harold Morton Landon Verse Translation Award from the American Academy of Poets for his translation of *Five Plays* by Heinrich von Keist, published by Yale University Press. His translation of Goethe's *Faust, Part One* is also published by Yale University Press.

"Part Two of Goethe's *Faust* is a sublimely outrageous poem, madly exuberant and endlessly inventive. Martin Greenberg's version catches the uncanny strangeness of Goethe's greatest work, and should help mediate it for American readers."—Harold Bloom, author of *Shakespeare: The Invention of the Human*

"There is no question that *Faust, Part Two* is the supreme poetic masterpiece of Germany's greatest writer. Its translation demands an almost unique commitment of effort and skill, and Greenberg's forceful, congenial version may truly be called the best available."
—Cyrus Hamlin, Yale University.

Praise For Greenburg's *Faust, Part One:*

"Greenberg has accomplished a magnificent literary feat. He has taken a great German work, until now all but inaccessible to English readers, and made it into a sparkling English poem, full of verve and wit. Greenberg's translation lives; it is done in a modern idiom but with respect for the original text; I found it a joy to read."
—Irving Howe

Yale University Press   New Haven and London